# ENGLISH, IRISH, and SCOTTISH FIREARMS MAKERS

# ENGLISH, IRISH, AND SCOTTISH FIREARMS MAKERS

### WHEN, WHERE, AND WHAT THEY MADE

### FROM THE MIDDLE OF THE SIXTEENTH CENTURY TO THE END OF THE NINETEENTH CENTURY

## A. MERWYN CAREY

ARCO PUBLISHING COMPANY, INC.

NEW YORK

Published by ARCO PUBLISHING COMPANY, Inc.
219 Park Avenue South, New York, N.Y. 10003

This edition is reproduced in facsimile from the original edition,
published 1954, by kind permission of Thomas Y. Crowell Company.

First edition, 1954
Second edition, 1967

Library of Congress Catalog Card Number 67-18414

Arco Catalog Number 1644

Printed in England

*To Edna*

Whose help, research, and encourage-
ment over the years made this book
possible—as in everything else.

# INTRODUCTION

COLLECTING THINGS OF long-ago generally falls into several phases: In the beginning, the collector is actuated by the pleasure of finding and possessing; after a time, this extends to a curiosity toward the more technical aspects, as represented by the evolution of form and decoration; and later, there is a strong urge to discover something of the history and work of individual makers.

Thus, the real collector eventually arrives at the stage of "digging" among old papers and documents in his search for facts relating to his interest; and having assembled a variety of odd bits of information, verified or discarded them, he quite frequently develops what Samuel Lover called "the itch of literature which nothing can cure but the scratching of a pen"; so an authoritative writer in a particular branch of antiques is born. Those of us interested in early crafts may be thankful collectors of different times have been affected by this aspiration, otherwise a mass of information now recorded would not be as easily available; for each successive generation has brought its quota of litterateur-connoisseurs to add something to these records.

Thus, "Doc" Carey, starting with only an average young man's interest in old firearms, has now given us what he aptly describes as a biographical cyclopedia of English, Irish, and Scottish makers of firearms. Over the past thirty-odd years, from many and varied sources, he has assembled the names of gunsmiths and a very considerable amount of detailed information concerning the more important men in the craft.

In one of my literary efforts, I quoted a favorite author of mine who had enjoyed an active and adventurous criminal past. One of his dictums was that an introduction was so much hot air unless it "told me something that mattered and helped me understand what comes after."

In other words, an introduction should be the appetizer. And "what comes after" in this book is not a conglomeration of pseudo-erudite jargon, sprinkled freely with clichés, but a compilation of data gathered over many years of studious research with the results verified in the light of the author's personal experience, as an unusually keen and observant collector; added to which is a deal of information garnered from British museums and dealers during his many annual visits to Britain, and further data culled from catalogues of sales held at the principal London auction rooms over the past quarter of a century.

Above, reference was made to the evolution of form and decoration. These aspects of firearms, particularly pistols, are of never-failing interest, even to a layman as distinct from an experienced collector. In both the form and the mechanism it is possible to follow the continuous effort of bygone gunsmiths to achieve more effective weapons; and in the decorative qualities, over the centuries, is something of man's cultural development expressed in the skill of the silversmith, the engraver and those artist-craftsmen who produced beauty by inlaying precious metals in steel.

For more years than my hoary head will now recall, it was my privilege to watch Merwyn Carey's collection increase; yea and, in my travels, to come upon some piece worthy of a place in it.

With the increase of his collection his interest in the history of firearms also increased and with it, his knowledge and understanding of the work of the early gunsmiths. That knowledge and understanding he now passes to other enthusiasts through the pages of this valuable addition to the literature of Firearms Makers.

EDWARD WENHAM

*Lympstone*
*Devon*
*England*

# *FOREWORD*

No BOOK ON English, Irish, and Scottish Firearms Makers will ever be complete. New evidence and new data is continually arising from old firearms and records that are being found from time to time. This book represents 33 years of careful and diligent research, collecting and inspecting old firearms. Its purpose is to help complete the record.

This is your book, your property, your basic record, and the format is such that your findings can be added under their proper classification. If you find a piece with a name that is not listed, and the markings of the maker are clear, and you have researched his place of fabrication and the years he made arms, then enter your findings under the proper listing.

Thus, ultimately, a more complete record is possible of English, Irish, and Scottish Firearms Makers.

A. MERWYN CAREY

GRATEFUL ACKNOWLEDGMENT

to

Herbert A. Sherlock for his arms drawings

and

for their helpful research
in the United Kingdom

Flight Lieut. M.T.C. Francis, R.A.F.V.R., of London
Major Ralph Judson M.B.E., F.R.A.S., of London
F. Horace Webber of Brighton, England
Edward Wenham of Lympstone, England

# CONTENTS

# LIST OF ILLUSTRATIONS

Following page 112

At page 116

**Abnett, William** [1790–1837] General gunsmith at Windsor, Berkshire.

**Achisone, Michael** [about 1660] Made all metal fishtail butt flintlock pistols at Doune, Scotland.

**Adams, Alexander** [1780–1810] Gunsmithery at London and Birmingham. Made flintlock rifles and double barrel flintlock pocket pistols and holster pistols. He also made screw barrel boxlock pocket flintlock pistols.

**Adams, Henry** [1850–1858] General gunsmith located at Gray's Inn Road, London.

**Adams, Joseph** [1767–1813] Gunsmithery located at Birmingham. Had Royal Government contract for flintlock holster pistols.

**Adams, Robert & John** (brothers) [1851–1892] Robert and John Adams patented a percussion revolver in 1851. These were made by **Deane, Adams & Deane** of 30 King William Street, London, with the plant in Southwark, London. They were solid frame, double-action, rotating cylinder with five chambers. Three types were made: The Dragoon .50 caliber, barrel 7½ or 8 inches. Navy .44 caliber, barrel 5¾ or 6¼ inches and Pocket .32 caliber, barrel 4½ inches. These were a direct trade challenge to Samuel Colt then manufacturing in London. In the spring of 1854 the Board of Ordnance tested both the Colt and Adams revolvers at Woolwich Arsenal and the decision was in favor of the Colt, on the basis of range and accuracy.

Deane, Adams and Deane bought the Beaumont Patent dated February 1855, which permitted either self-cocking (single action) or double action thus having the Colt feature of single action. **Deane, Adams & Deane** dissolved in 1856 and the Adams Patents were taken over by the **London Armoury Company** in which Robert and John Adams and John Kerr were co-directors. (John Kerr, a London gunsmith under the name of John Kerr & Co.) Kerr's patent was a compound rammer built in the side of the frame alongside the barrel. In 1857 after a series of Board of Ordnance field trials the Beaumont–Adams percussion revolver was adapted by the War Office for all branches of the British Service and gained popularity in the Indian Mutiny.

John Adams co-director of the London Armoury Company patented in October 1867, a metallic cartridge revolver with side ejector and this was adapted by the Ordnance Board to replace the Beaumont–Adams percussion revolver. Shortly after this date John Adams severed his association with the **London Armoury Company** and formed the **Adams Patent Small Arms Company** at 391 Strand, London, with plant at 9 Finsbury Place, London. This company made center fire metallic cartridge revolvers of .45 and .38 caliber. The firm closed in 1892.

**Adcock, G. T.** [1861–1878] General gunsmith in London.

**Addis, Thomas** [1629–1635] One of the seven gunsmiths in London whose name appeared in the text of a commission granted by Charles I to make Royal arms.

**Addison, Thomas** [about 1690] Gunsmithery in London, probably son of Thomas Addis.

**Adge, Richard** [about 1765] General gunsmith in Birmingham.

**Ager, Wilson & Co.** [about 1865] Custom gunsmiths and dealers in London.

**Aislabie** [1740–1750] Located in London, general gunsmith.

**Akrill, H.** [about 1850] Made percussion sporting rifles at Beverly, Yorkshire.

**Alard Fils, H.** [1890–1900] Custom gunsmith, dealer and importer in London.

**Alden & Smith** [about 1860] General gunsmiths and dealers in London.

**Aldrige, George** [about 1715] Established a gunsmithery in London.

**Alison** [about 1585] Made all metal fishtail butt snaphaunce pistols at Dundee, Scotland.

**Allan** [about 1800] Made flintlock wild fowl punt gun and did general gunsmithing at Ashford, Kent.

**Allan, William** [1740–1800] Gunsmithery located at Edinburgh, Scotland. Made flintlock all metal steel pistols with scroll butts.

**Allcorn** [about 1770] Had Royal Government contract for flintlock carbines at London.

**Allely** [1820–1840] Shop at 5 Great Portland Street, London. Made percussion sporting guns and big-game "Howdah Pistol" large caliber with tube lock.

**Allen, R.** [1710–1750] Located at Birmingham and London. Made Queen Anne–type flintlock pocket pistols, brass barrel flintlock blunderbusses and flintlock fowling pieces.

**Alley, George** [1780–1810] General gunsmith at Dublin, Ireland.

**Alley, L.** [1710–1775] Made Queen Anne–type boxlock flintlock pistols and double barrel flintlock holster pistols at Dublin, Ireland.

**Alley, W.** [about 1790] Shop located at Kilkenny, Ireland. Made flintlock duelling pistols.

**Allez, N.** [about 1760] General gunsmith at Dublin, Ireland.

**Allot** [about 1830] Shop located at Barnsley, Yorkshire. General gunsmith.

**Allport, Henry** [1830–1840] Made cased percussion traveling pistols with all accessories, at Cork, Ireland.

**Allport, H. S. & Thomas F.** [about 1890] Custom gunmakers in London.

**Allport, J.** [1770–1800] Made screw barrel flintlock pocket pistols, flintlock carbines with brass mountings, and flintlock rifles. Shop in London.

**Allport, Thomas** [1809–1815] Shop at Birmingham. Made cased flintlock duelling pistols.

**Allport, William** [1813–1825] Made brass barrel flintlock naval pistols at Birmingham.

**Ancell, Robert** [1800–1830] Shop at Perth, Scotland. Made all metal, scroll butt flintlock pistols with sash or belt hook. Name changed to **Ancell & Salmond,** located on George Street, Perth, Scotland, from 1830 to 1850. Made percussion pocket pistols with silver mountings and double barrel percussion sporting guns.

**Anderson** [1800–1813] General gunsmith at Birmingham.

**Anderson, John** [about 1800] Shop at Malton, Yorkshire. General gunsmith.

**Anderson, Robert** [1825–1835] General gunsmith in London.

**Andrews** [1780–1810] Made flintlock traveling pistols, with silver mountings, shop in London.

**Andrews, Benjamin** [about 1835] General gunsmith at Ross, Hertfordshire.

**Andrews, C. W.** [1850–1882] Made percussion naval pistols with belt hooks, also percussion holster and pocket pistols. Shop in London.

**Anens, S.** [about 1690] Established a gunsmithery in London.

**Anglin** [about **1850**] General gunsmith at Wexford, Ireland.

**Annely, L.** [**1650–1700**] Made flintlock screw barrel pocket pistols in London.

**Annely, T.** [about **1720**] Shop in London. Made brass barrel flintlock holster pistols and flintlock blunderbusses.

**Antley, John** [about **1865**] Custom gunmaker in London.

**Appleton, Henry M.** [**1869–1875**] General gunsmith in London.

**Archer, Thomas Sr. & Jr.** [**1780–1810**] Made cannon barrel boxlock flintlock pocket pistols, and flintlock holster pistols, also brass barrel flintlock blunderbusses. Shop in Birmingham. Trade name **Thomas Archer & Son** 1812 to 1818.

**Archer, William** [**1750–1790**] Shop in London. Made brass cannon barrel boxlock flintlock pocket pistols and boxlock flintlock traveling pistols with ivory butt stock. Also brass barrel flintlock blunderbusses.

**Arden, W.** [**1710–1730**] General gunsmith in London and Dublin, Ireland. Made cannon barrel flintlock coach pistols.

**Armbruster** [about **1860**] Shop in London. General gunsmith.

**Armstrong** [**1820–1840**] Made percussion holster pistols at Clonmel, Ireland.

**Ash, Samuel** [**1797–1808**] General gunsmith in London.

**Ashmore** [about **1699**] Established a gunsmithery in London.

**Ashmore, R.** [**1768–1775**] Made flintlock holster pistols in London.

**Ashton** [**1780–1800**] Shop at Romford, Essex. Made brass barrel flintlock blunderbuss type pistols and flintlock naval pistols with belt hook.

**Ashton, T.** [**1840–1858**] General gunsmith in London.

**Aspinal, T.** [about **1810**] Shop in Birmingham. General gunsmith.

**Aspinall** [**1760–1800**] Made double superimposed barrels, boxlock flintlock coach pistols in London.

**Aston, John H.** [about **1850**] General gunsmith in Birmingham.

**Aston, Richard & William** [about **1865**] Shop in London, general gunsmiths.

**Aston, Thomas** [about **1810**] Made flintlock pocket pistol with spring bayonet. Shop at Birmingham.

**Aston, W.** [**1780–1820**] Shop at Manchester, Lancashire. Made brass barrel flintlock blunderbusses.

**Atkin, Henry** [**1862–1877**] Made large bore, wild fowl percussion guns for swivel on boat. Shop located at Chelsea, London.

**Atkin & Co., Henry E.** [**1874–1900**] Dealers and custom gunmakers at 88 Jermyn Street, London.

**Atwood, T.** [**1830–1840**] General gunsmith in London.

**Auchinleck, John** [about **1630**] Did gunsmithing in Scotland, location unknown.

**Austin, Jacob** [about **1692**] Established a gunsmithery in Birmingham.

**Austin, T.** [**1688–1720**] Made flintlock carbines with Royal Cypher.

**Ayers, J.** [about **1800**] General gunsmith at Newbury, Berkshire.

# NOTES

## A

**Babwick** [about **1780**] Made screw barrel boxlock, folding trigger flintlock pocket pistols at Norwich, Norfolk.

**Backhouse, I.** [**1690–1710**] Made Queen Anne–type screw barrel flintlock pocket pistols in London.

**Bacon, Benjamin** [about **1775**] General gunsmith in London.

**Bagley, John** [about **1810**] Shop in Birmingham. General gunsmith.

**Bagnall, Robert** [about **1770**] General gunsmith in Birmingham.

**Bailes** [**1720–1750**] Made flintlock fowling pieces at Oxford.

**Bailes, W.** [about **1760**] Shop in London. Made flintlock coach pistols with silver mask butt caps.

**Bailey** [**1750–1759**] General gunsmith at Newark upon Trent, Nottingham.

**Bailey** [about **1835**] Made sawhandle percussion duelling pistols at Maidenhead, Berkshire.

**Bailey, J.** [**1775–1800**] Shop in London. Made cannon barrel boxlock flintlock pocket pistols with silver mask butt caps.

**Bailey, T.** [about **1830**] General gunsmith at Stamford, Lincolnshire.

**Baker, Ezekiel** [**1775–1832**] Ezekiel Baker, one of the famous London gunsmiths, was apprenticed and learned his trade under Henry Nock, and in 1775 established his own gunshop at 24 Whitechapel Road. His production over the years included a number of Royal Government contracts for flintlock muskets, rifles, carbines, and pistols. His custom work, for which he had the Royal Warrant, included fowling pieces, cased duelling pistols and blunderbusses. He also had numerous contracts with the East India Company for their arms. In the later years he made percussion arms in the above categories.

On February 4, 1800, at Woolwich Arsenal he competed with several European, American, and English gunsmiths before the Honorable Board of Ordnance for a flintlock muzzle-loading rifle contract for the British Army. He was awarded this contract and the 95th Regiment of the British Army, later called the Rifle Brigade, were issued these rifles and were the first line regiment to use rifles in the Army. Colonel Patrick Ferguson's breech-loading flintlock rifle (a few were made by Baker) were used some years earlier in the War of Independence but these were used by a regiment of Loyalist Riflemen.

In 1803 after extensive field trials Baker was awarded a Board of Ordnance contract for flintlock rifled carbines, these were issued to the 10th Regiment, the Bedfordshire Light Dragoons. On May 15, 1806, Baker conducted tests at Woolwich Arsenal of heavy rifled wall pieces but these were not practical and no contract was awarded. In 1816 he was commissioned by the East India Company and made several improvements on the flintlock muskets, carbines, and pistols of the Company; namely, raised the flashpan and grooved it so water could not penetrate the priming, improved the spring on the bayonet and made it more secure, thus saved one motion in the manual of arms putting on and taking off the bayonet.

In 1821 he patented a new bullet mold and clipper for casting balls by which the ball was cast more solid and the neck or gate was clipped off, leaving the ball perfectly round. In 1822 he made improvements of the jaws and comb of the hammer of the flintlock, which gave greater purchase to the flint and made the flint a simpler operation. These improvements were all adapted in his Royal Government contracts. In 1824 Baker perfected a lock that could be used both as a flintlock or percussion lock with the necessary barrel touchhole attachment.

Ezekiel Baker also established under Crown Grant a proof house adjoining the premises at 24 Whitechapel Road, which was the first individual gunmaker's proof house. The two others in London being the Government Proof House at the Tower of London and the Gunmakers Guild Proof House on Commercial Road. In 1821 Baker published a "chart of the weight and diameter of Lead Balls" which with "a table showing the number in one ounce and in one pound" are still considered today the authority among collectors. With his close association with the East India Company he made a number of big-game heavy caliber rifles both flintlock and percussion.

Ezekiel Baker died in 1832 and the firm was carried on under the name of **E. Baker & Son** from 1833 to 1853.

**Baker, Frederick T.** [1830–1840] Made double barrel percussion shotguns at Birmingham.

**Baker, J.** [1640–1650] Established gunsmithery in London.

**Baker, Thomas K.** [1851–1890] General gunsmith at 88 Fleet Street, London. Patented a single-action percussion revolver dated April 24, 1852.

**Balchin** [1830–1840] Made percussion pocket pistols at Hull, Yorkshire.

**Bales, G. W.** [1780–1820] Shop at Ipswich, Suffolk. Made flintlock fowling pieces.

**Bales & King** [about 1825] General gunsmiths in London.

**Ball** [about 1820] Made brass barrel flintlock holster pistols in London.

**Bankes** [1685–1689] Made flintlock carbines with Royal Cypher in London.

**Banks** [about 1860] General gunsmith at Chippenham, Wiltshire.

**Barbar, I.** [1740–1780] Made Queen Anne–type, cannon barrel flintlock pocket pistols with silver mounts, brass mounted flintlock holster pistols, brass barrel blunderbuss-type flintlock coach pistols and flintlock fowling pieces. Shop at Shoe Lane, London. His pieces were marked "Londini."

**Barbar, L.** [1720–1750] Shop in London. Made brass cannon barrel flintlock coach pistols and flintlock holster pistols.

**Barbar, T.** [1770–1800] Shop at Newark, Nottingham. General gunsmith.

**Barker** [about 1720] General gunsmith at Newark, Nottingham.

**Barker & Harris** [about 1770] Shop in Birmingham, general gunsmiths.

**Barker, W.** [1770–1780] General gunsmith at Wigan, Lancashire.

**Barn, John** [1708–1714] Shop in London, general gunsmith.

**Barne, Harman** [1635–1670] Gunmaker to Prince Rupert at the time of the Civil Wars. Made one of the earliest known breech-loading flintlock rifles. By pressing the trigger guard, the barrel hinged from the stock to the left. Shop in London. (Used "Londini" in marking his pieces.)

**Barnes, Frederick** [1850–1890] Made percussion musketoons and percussion double barrel naval pistols with belt hook, under Royal Government contract. For the civilian trade made double barrel, over and under, large caliber percussion sporting rifles and percussion revolvers. Shop in London.

**Barnett, Thomas** [1750–1800] Thomas Barnett was the founder of a dynasty of gunmakers in London. Made flintlock fowling pieces and under Royal Government contract made flintlock musketoons and flintlock pistols for the Revenue Customs Service. The firm name was **Barnett & Son 1800 to 1835**. They made brass barrel flintlock blunderbusses for the East India Company and "Trade" flintlock muskets and rifles for the Hudson's Bay Company. The name changed to **John Barnett & Sons** 1835 to 1875 when under Royal Government contract they made percussion sea-service pistols and muskets with brass mountings. The name from 1875 to 1900 was **Edward Barnett & Sons.**

**Barton, John** [1790–1820] Made cased flintlock duelling and holster pistols and silver mounted flintlock pocket pistols in London.

**Barton, L.** [1810–1820] General gunsmith in London.

**Barton, T.** [1825–1830] Made cased flintlock duelling pistols with all accessories, in London.

**Barwick** [1775–1810] Shop in London. Made brass barrel flintlock holster pistols and double barrel flintlock fowling pieces.

**Bass** [1770–1780] Made flintlock pocket, coach, and duelling pistols in London. Firm name became **Twigg & Bass** in 1780.

**Bate, Thomas** [1770–1810] Established both in London and Birmingham. Made screw barrel flintlock pistols and cased flintlock duelling pistols; also flintlock fowling pieces with silver mountings and fine workmanship.

**Bateman, Robert** [about 1835] General gunsmith at Thirsk, Yorkshire.

**Bates** [1825–1850] Shops at Ipswich, Suffolk, and Colchester, Essex. Made naval percussion pistols with belt hook.

**Bates, Job** [about 1835] General gunsmith at Richmond, Yorkshire.

**Bates, John** [1810–1825] Made flintlock holster pistols in London.

**Baussart, G.** [about 1740] Shop in London. Made steel barrel flintlock holster pistols.

**Bawdes, Thomas** [about 1677] Established a gunsmithery in London.

**Bayley, J.** [1770–1800] Made steel barrel flintlock blunderbusses and flintlock holster pistols in London.

**Bayliss & Son, E.** [about 1870] Custom gunmakers and dealers in London.

**Bays, Thomas** [about 1785] Shop in London. General gunsmith.

**Bear, Robert** [about 1643] Had gunsmithery in Scotland. Location not known.

**Beary** [about 1750] General gunsmith in London.

**Beasley, Benjamin** [about 1865] Shop located in London. General gunsmith.

**Beattie, James** [1835–1865] Located at 205 Regent Street, London. Made boxlock percussion pocket pistols with folding trigger of fine workmanship, percussion pepperboxes, also percussion naval pistol with swivel ramrod and belt hook. Name changed to **J. Beattie & Son** 1865 to 1879 at same address. Made percussion, over and under barrel, pistols with two hammers and two triggers, and percussion double-action revolver of Tranter Patents. Name became **Beattie & Co.** from 1879 to 1894.

**Beck, T.** [about 1830] General gunsmith at Bridgwater, Somerset.

**Beckett** [about 1770] Shop located in St. James, London.

**Beckwith, H.** [1790–1830] Made steel barrel flintlock holster pistols in Birmingham.

**Beckwith, William A.** [1840–1870] Made percussion pepperboxes and a percussion four-barrel revolving carbine on pepperbox principal; also boxlock percussion pocket pistols, and cased percussion revolver with all accessories. Shop in London.

**Beddowes, John** [about 1825] General gunsmith in London.

**Bedford Bros.** [about 1865] Shop in London. General gunsmith.

**Bees** [about 1800] General gunsmith at Bristol, Gloucestershire.

**Beesley, Frederic** [1879–1900] Custom gunmaker in London. Merged with Stephen Grant and Joseph Lang, Ltd. in 1900.

**Bell, D.** [1827–1840] Shop at York. General gunsmith.

**Benjamin & Burler** [1861–1872] Custom gunmakers and dealers in London, became **Henry Benjamin** 1872 to 1882.

**Bennet** [about 1850] Made cased percussion traveling pistols at Southampton.

**Bennet** [about 1800] Shop in Birmingham. Made brass barrel flintlock blunderbusses.

**Bennett** [1771–1805] Made flintlock duelling pistols, silver mounted brass barrel flintlock coach pistols, also presentation officers' flintlock holster pistols. All of fine workmanship. Shop at Royal Exchange, London.

**Benson, T.** [about 1760] General gunsmith in London.

**Bentley, John** [1852–1885] Patented in 1852 a percussion revolver with a spring safety catch fitted on head of the hammer which held the hammer clear of the cap and nipples. These patent rights he turned over to Philip Webley in 1853 to be used on the new Webley percussion revolver. Bentley made saw-handle percussion duelling pistols and percussion pepperboxes. Some of the .44 caliber double-action percussion revolvers he made had a spring bayonet on the side of the barrel. His shop was in London and the firm name became **Bentley & Playfair** from 1885 to 1900.

**Bentley & Son** [1857–1873] Custom gunmakers and dealers in Liverpool. Made cased .44 caliber percussion revolvers with accessories.

**Berry** [about 1840] Made percussion pepperboxes at Woodbridge, Suffolk.

**Bevington, A.** [1880–1890] Custom gunmaker in London.

**Bicknell, A.** [1660–1680] Shop in London, general gunsmith.

**Bidet** [1721–1731] Emigrated from France and established a gunsmithery in London (used "Londini" in marking his pieces). Made a breech-loading flintlock fowling piece with a screw breech turned by the trigger guard. (This piece may have given Major Patrick Ferguson the idea for his breech-loading flintlock rifle.) Bidet's piece was 52 inches over all with a 37-inch barrel and a bore of ⅝ inches. Steel mountings etched with foliage and huntsmen. The escutcheon plate bore the arms of George I of England.

**Biggs, F. T.** [1876–1886] Custom gunmaker in London.

**Biglan** [about 1785] General gunsmith in Dublin, Ireland.

**Biken, I.** [1680–1690] Made flintlock fowling pieces and flintlock muskets with the Royal Cypher. Shop located in London.

**Bingham, John** [about **1815**] General gunsmith in Birmingham.

**Binney** [about **1775**] Made cannon barrel flintlock pocket pistols in London.

**Bircham, Charles O.** [**1867–1900**] Custom gunmaker in London, specialized in percussion and metallic cartridge sporting rifles.

**Birchett, Edward** [**1700–1713**] Made steel barrel flintlock coach pistols with silver mountings and flintlock holster pistols. Shop in London.

**Bird** [about **1800**] Shop in London. Made cased flintlock duelling pistols.

**Bishop, J.** [**1800–1820**] Made screw barrel flintlock pocket pistols and flintlock duelling pistols, also flintlock fowling pieces in London.

**Bissel, Isaac** [**1745–1780**] Shop in Birmingham. Made Scottish-type all metal flintlock pistols with scroll or ramshorn butt, also brass barrel flintlock naval pistols with Royal Cypher.

**Bissel, Thomas** [**1857–1891**] Custom gunmaker in London.

**Bissell** [**1740–1770**] Made all metal flintlock pistols with scroll butt. Shop in Leith, Scotland.

**Biven, A. F.** [**1830–1842**] Shop at Waterloo Place, London. Made double barrel percussion sporting guns.

**Black, James** [about **1835**] General gunsmith at Berwick, Scotland.

**Black, William** [about **1625**] Established a gunsmithery in Scotland. Location not known.

**Blaikie** [about **1800**] Made double barrel flintlock fowling pieces at Addington, Kent.

**Blair** [**1770–1800**] Boxlock flintlock pocket pistols with folding trigger, cannon barrel flintlock traveling pistols, and flintlock holster pistols. Shop in London.

**Blair & Co.** [**1830–1850**] Made percussion duelling pistols at Birmingham.

**Blake** [**1770–1790**] Made brass cannon barrel boxlock flintlock traveling pistols, flintlock holster pistols, and flintlock fowling pieces at London.

**Blake, John Alkin** [**1825–1864**] Shop located in Wapping, London. Made percussion pepperboxes and double barrel percussion naval pistols. Also cased double barrel sporting guns with all accessories. Specialized in large bore percussion swivel boat shotgun for commercial water fowl shooting.

**Blakely** [about **1860**] General gunsmith in Birmingham.

**Blakemore** [**1775–1790**] Shop in Birmingham. General gunsmith.

**Blakemore, V. & A.** [**1867–1895**] Custom gunmakers in London.

**Blanch, John** [**1800–1835**] Made boxlock flintlock pocket pistols at Hull, Yorkshire.

**Blanch, W. H.** [about **1870**] Custom gunmaker and dealer at 4 Berry Square, Liverpool.

**Blanche, John** [**1809–1835**] Made bell muzzle, flintlock pocket pistols with under spring bayonet, and lightweight flintlock cadet muskets. Shop at 29 Grace Church Street, London. Name changed to **John Blanche & Son** at same address 1835 to 1865. Under this name made percussion pepperboxes, cased percussion traveling pistols with swivel ramrod and fittings. Also percussion revolvers, Tranter Patent.

**Blanckley, J.** [**1640–1688**] Shop in London. Made brass barrel flintlock blunderbusses.

**Bland & Sons, Thomas** [**1840–1895**] Custom gunmakers and dealers at 4

& 5 King William Street, Strand, London.

**Blight, Richard** [about **1780**] General gunsmith in London.

**Blisset, I.** [**1800–1830**] Made double barrel flintlock holster pistols with spring bayonet. Located at 69 Leadenhall Street, London.

**Blissett, John** [**1840–1877**] Shops at 316 High Holborn, London, and South Cassel Street, Liverpool. Made percussion pepperboxes, officers' percussion dragoon pistols with swivel ramrod and double barrel percussion pocket pistols. Name changed to **Blissett Sons & Tomes** (London address only) 1877 to 1883.

**Blissett, Thomas** [**1837–1864**] Made percussion naval pistols with belt or sash hook. Shop located in London.

**Blyth, Henry** [**1710–1750**] Made Queen Anne–type flintlock pocket pistols, and flintlock greatcoat pocket pistols of blunderbuss type. Shop in London. Name became **Blyth & Co.** 1750 to 1790. Made flintlock holster pistols and flintlock muskets with Tower Proof and Royal Cypher.

**Boaler** [about **1780**] Made flintlock blunderbusses with under spring bayonet. Shop in London.

**Boales, T.** [about **1830**] General gunsmith at Newark, Nottinghamshire.

**Bodley, Thomas** [about **1677**] Established a gunsmithery in London.

**Boles, Thomas** [about **1770**] Shop in Birmingham. General gunsmith.

**Bollin** [about **1770**] Made screw barrel flintlock pocket pistols in London.

**Bolton, F. H. & George** [**1773–1800**] George Bolton invented a flintlock action which had a screwless lock plate and the hammer or cock was inside

the lock plate. Made brass barrel flintlock pistols of the blunderbuss-type with under spring bayonet. Shop in London.

**Bolton, James** [about **1805**] General gunsmith in Birmingham.

**Bolton, Peter** [about **1715**] Made brass barrel flintlock holster pistols in London.

**Bolton, Richard** [about **1815**] Shop in Birmingham. General gunsmith.

**Bolton, Thomas** [**1776–1813**] Made boxlock flintlock pocket pistols with folding triggers. Shop in London.

**Bond, G. E.** [about **1820**] General gunsmith in Thetford, Norfolk.

**Bond, William** [**1768–1776**] William Bond was the founder of a famous family of gunsmiths in London and was active in gunsmithing until 1776. From 1776 to 1800 **Philip Bond** had a shop at 45 Cornhill, London. Made brass barrel flintlock pocket pistols with under spring bayonet, and flintlock blunderbusses with spring bayonet. **Edward Bond** at 45 Cornhill, London, was active from 1800 to 1830. Made flintlock holster pistols with swivel ramrod and double barrel flintlock carbines with top spring bayonets. **William Bond** was located at 59 Lombard Street, London, from 1830 to 1850. Made cased percussion traveling pistols of fine workmanship. **Edward William Bond** (probably son of William) was active 1850 to 1861. Made cased percussion pepperboxes. **Edward Philip Bond** was active 1861 to 1870 and **Edward William Bond** (probably **Junior**) from 1870 to 1879.

**Bonehill, C. S.** [about **1880**] Made double barrel breech-loading cartridge shotguns. Located in Birmingham.

**Bonell, A.** [about **1850**] Shop in London. Made cased percussion pepperboxes.

**Bonney, George** [about 1850] Made boxlock flintlock coach pistols with silver mask butt caps. Did gunsmithing at Preston, Lancashire.

**Bonstead, Frederick** [1825–1838] General gunsmith in London.

**Boot, Richard** [about 1810] Shop in Birmingham. General gunsmith.

**Booth, Robert** [about 1840] General gunsmith in Sunderland, Durham.

**Boowles, R.** [about 1690] Made flintlock holster pistols in London.

**Borle, John** [about 1770] Shop in Birmingham. General gunsmith.

**Boss, Thomas** [1850–1870] Custom gunmaker and dealer in London. Made percussion pepperboxes and cased percussion traveling pistols. Name became **Boss & Co.** at 41 Albemarle Street, Piccadilly, London, 1870.

**Boston, John** [about 1835] General gunsmith at Wakefield, Yorkshire.

**Boswell, Charles** [1880–1900] Shop at 15 Strafford Road, London. Custom gunmaker.

**Bosworth, John** [about 1865] General gunsmith in London.

**Bott & Son** [about 1890] Custom gunmakers in London.

**Bourdeveaux, Peter** [about 1850] Gunsmith, dealer and importer in London.

**Bourne, Joseph** [1840–1883] Shops in London and Birmingham. Made percussion revolver, Tranter Patent, and over and under metallic cartridge express rifles of .50 caliber. Name became **Joseph Bourne & Son** 1883 to 1900.

**Bowdler, L.** [about 1800] Made double barrel flintlock pocket pistols, also flintlock duelling pistols. Shop located in Shropshire.

**Bowley, Berthon** [about 1760] Shop in London, also a shop at Malta. Made officers' flintlock holster pistols.

**Boyton, S.** [about 1780] General gunsmith in London.

**Bozard & Co.** [1880–1899] Custom gunmakers in London.

**Braddell, J.** [about 1860] Made cased pair of double-action percussion revolvers at Belfast, Ireland.

**Bradford** [about 1800] Shop in London. Made screw barrel flintlock pocket pistols.

**Bradney, W.** [about 1780] Made boxlock flintlock pocket pistols with folding trigger, in London.

**Bragg** [about 1855] Shop located at 57 High Holborn, London. Made percussion holster pistols with swivel ramrod.

**Braithwaite, John** [about 1835] General gunsmith at Leeds, Yorkshire.

**Brander, W.** (3 generations) [1690–1750] Shop located in the Minories, London. Made brass barrel flintlock carbine for the East India Company and flintlock coach pistols. For the next two generations known as **W. B. Brander** in the Minories from 1750 to 1825 and they had extensive Royal Government contracts for flintlock holster pistols and flintlock muskets. The name changed to **Brander & Potts** at 70 Minories with another shop at Winchelsea, from 1825 to 1832.

**Brandon, Joel B.** [1870–1877] Custom gunmaker in London.

**Brasher, John** [1800–1835] Shops in both London and Birmingham. Made three-barrel flintlock pocket pistols and flintlock holster pistols. Later made cased percussion traveling pistols and percussion sporting guns.

**Brass** [about 1850] Made cased percussion duelling pistols at High Holborn, London.

**Brazier, T. R.** [about **1855**] Made percussion revolver (Brazier Patent), cased with fittings, at Wolverhampton, Staffordshire.

**Brewer, Eugene G.** [**1877–1885**] Custom gunmaker in London.

**Brewster, William** [about **1835**] Shop at Long Stratton, Norfolk. Made percussion sporting rifles.

**Briden, George** [about **1855**] General gunsmith in London.

**Bridgens, Thomas** [about **1770**] Shop in Birmingham. General gunsmith.

**Bridgewater** [about **1820**] General gunsmith in London.

**Bridle** [about **1790**] Shop in London. General gunsmith.

**Brielton** [about **1770**] General gunsmith in London.

**Briscoe** [about **1810**] Made double barrel flintlock fowling pieces of fine workmanship. Shop located in London.

**Brompton** [**1785–1800**] Shop in Doncaster, Yorkshire. Made flintlock fowling pieces.

**Brooke, Benjamin** [**1680–1720**] Made cannon barrel flintlock coach pistols with silver mask butt caps. Shop in London.

**Brooke, John Sr. & Jr.** [about **1715**] Shop in London. Made cannon barrel flintlock pocket pistols.

**Brooke, R.** [**1640–1700**] Made flintlock carbines and muskets with the Royal Cypher. Shop in London.

**Brooks** [about **1750**] Shop in Dublin, Ireland. Made brass barrel flintlock blunderbusses.

**Brooks, Benjamin** [about **1710**] Made Queen Anne–type flintlock coach pistols and flintlock fowling pieces. Shop located in London.

**Brooks, J. & R.** [about **1686**] Established a gunsmithery in London. Made brass barrel flintlock holster pistols.

**Brooks & Son, Edward** [**1810–1830**] Made brass barrel flintlock blunderbusses in Birmingham.

**Broom** [about **1820**] Shop in London. Made pairs of screw barrel flintlock pocket pistols with folding triggers.

**Broomhead & Watson** [about **1750**] Made Queen Anne–type boxlock flintlock pocket pistols in London.

**Brown** [about **1840**] Custom gunmaker in Glasgow, Scotland.

**Brown, John** [**1810–1830**] Shop at 140 Strand, London. Made cased flintlock duelling pistols.

**Brown, Thomas** [**1803–1825**] General gunsmith at Newcastle upon Tyne, Northumberland.

**Brown & Mannett** [about **1865**] Custom gunmakers in London.

**Bruce, George** [about **1650**] Established a gunsmithery in Scotland, location not known.

**Brueton** [about **1780**] General gunsmith in London.

**Bruie, Henry** [about **1855**] Custom gunmaker in London.

**Brumfield** [about **1760**] Shop in London. General gunsmith.

**Brummitt, Samuel** [**1770–1820**] Made double barrel, over and under, flintlock pocket pistols and double barrel flintlock fowling pieces of fine workmanship. Also made flintlock rifles. Shop located at Warsop, Nottinghamshire.

**Brunn, S.** [1780–1835] Shop at 55 Charing Cross, London. Held the Royal Warrant to the Prince Regent in 1800. Made screw barrel flintlock pocket pistols with folding trigger and flintlock coach pistols, also flintlock duelling and holster pistols. Later made percussion naval pistols with belt hook.

**Brunton, R.** [1800–1822] Made screw barrel flintlock pocket pistols with folding trigger, and flintlock holster pistols. Shop at York.

**Brush, John** [1700–1714] General gunsmith in London.

**Brush, R.** [1701–1709] Made flintlock muskets with Royal Cypher in London.

**Bryan** [about 1770] Made cased saw-handle flintlock duelling pistols at Cork, Ireland.

**Bryce, Edmund** [about 1850] Made steel and silver percussion dress pistols with scroll butt. Shop in Edinburgh, Scotland.

**Brydon, William** [1775–1800] Shop in Edinburgh. Made flintlock holster pistols with walnut stock and butts.

**Buchan** [about 1800] Made brass frame flintlock pistols with scroll butt. Shop in Dundee, Scotland.

**Buckley, Thomas** [about 1800] General gunsmith at Birmingham.

**Buckmaster, J.** [1720–1770] Made brass cannon barrel flintlock coach pistols. Shop in London.

**Bucks** [about 1750] Under Royal Government contract made flintlock Yeoman of the Guard pistols. Shop in London.

**Budding** [about 1840] Made five-barrel percussion pepperbox. This was hand turned. Shop in London.

**Bull, Thomas** [1790–1841] General gunsmith in Bedford.

**Bulleid, T.** [about 1830] Shop at Bristol, Gloucestershire. General gunsmith.

**Bulman, Thomas** [about 1790] General gunsmith at Newcastle upon Tyne, Northumberland.

**Bumford, I.** [1720–1776] Made brass cannon barrel, boxlock flintlock coach pistols with mask butt caps. Shop located in London.

**Bunday, Joseph** [about 1715] General gunsmith in London.

**Bunn, William** [about 1860] Shop located in London. Custom gunmaker.

**Bunney, Joseph** (3 generations: father, son, grandson) [1730–1815] Made brass cannon barrel boxlock flintlock pocket and coach pistols, and flintlock holster pistols with Royal Cypher; also cased flintlock duelling pistols with all accessories. Shops in London and Birmingham.

**Burbach** [1706–1716] General gunsmith in London.

**Buresh, F.** [about 1815] Shop in London. General gunsmith.

**Burges, John** [1700–1720] Made all metal flintlock pistols with heart-shaped butt. Shop in Elgin, Scotland.

**Burgon, William** [1715–1750] Shop in London. Made double barrel side-by-side flintlock naval pistols with top spring bayonet.

**Burnand, Richard** [1800–1840] Made cased flintlock traveling pistols with silver mountings. Shop at Newcastle upon Tyne. William Greener was apprenticed to and learned his trade with Richard Burnand.

**Burnell, John** [1820–1840] General gunsmith at South Street, Taunton, Somerset.

**Burnett** [1810–1840] Shop in Southampton. Made cased flintlock duelling pistols and later percussion naval pistols.

**Burnie, M.** [about **1810**] Shop in Berwick, Scotland. Made cannon barrel flintlock pocket pistols with wood butts.

**Burrow** [about **1850**] Made percussion sporting rifles at Bristol, Gloucestershire.

**Burrowe, Richard** [**1613–1631**] One of the seven gunsmiths in London whose name appeared in a text of a commission granted by Charles I to make Royal arms.

**Burrows, Edwin** [about **1875**] Custom gunmaker in London.

**Burrows, G. & J.** [**1820–1840**] Shop at 116 Fishergate, Preston, Lancashire. Made cased, swivel ramrod, percussion pistols of fine workmanship.

**Burtinshaw, William** [about **1835**] General gunmaker in Manchester.

**Burton, T. H.** [about **1865**] Shop in London. Custom gunmaker.

**Busby** [**1813–1820**] Made boxlock flintlock pocket pistols, in London.

**Bussey & Co., G.** [**1870–1889**] Custom gunmakers in London.

**Butler** [about **1780**] Shop at Christ Church, Southampton. Made boxlock flintlock pocket pistols.

**Buttall, J.** [**1720–1770**] General gunsmith in London.

**Button, Charles Pomeroy** [about **1840**] Shop at 142 Cheapside, London. General gunsmith.

**Bye, Samuel** [about **1715**] General gunsmith in London.

**Byrne, Charles** [about **1775**] Shop in London. General gunsmith.

# NOTES
## B

**Caddell, Thomas** [1646–1678] Thomas Caddell was the first to establish a gunsmithery in Doune, Perthshire, Scotland. He also established a succession of famous craftsmen and makers of the Scottish-type of all metal snaphaunce and flintlock pistols. His son Thomas, Jr., carried on the shop in Doune from 1678 to 1718 and two generations of the family followed him from 1718 to 1775. Robert Caddell, son of Thomas, Jr., established a shop in Edinburgh and was active from 1730 to 1764.

**Cadiot, Emanuel H.** [about 1875] Custom gunmaker and importer in London.

**Cairns** [about 1760] Shop in Birmingham. General gunsmith.

**Caius & Fearn** [about 1790] General gunsmiths in Manchester.

**Calderwood** [about 1800] Shop in London. General gunsmith.

**Calderwood** [1815–1860] Shop in Dublin, Ireland. Made brass barrel flintlock blunderbusses and pairs of brass barrel flintlock holster pistols to match. These were used by guards on the Royal mail coaches in Ireland. Later made cased percussion duelling pistols with all accessories and percussion revolvers of Adams Patent.

**Calisher & Terry** [1855–1870] Shops in Birmingham and at 28 Norfolk Street, London. Under Royal Government contract made percussion breech-loading carbines used by the British cavalry 1857 to 1861. Also made a percussion breech-loading pistol of the Terry Patent.

**Calvert** [about 1810] General gunsmith in London.

**Calvert, T. W.** [1810–1850] Shop at Leeds, Yorkshire. Made boxlock flintlock pocket and coach pistols. Later cased pairs of percussion duelling pistols with loading equipment and single-action percussion revolvers.

**Cameron, Alexander** [1725–1755] Made steel flintlock pistols with scroll butt at Edinburgh, Scotland.

**Campbell, Alexander** [1725–1775] All metal flintlock pistols with scroll butt. Shop at Doune, Perthshire, Scotland.

**Campbell, John** (3 generations) [1710–1798] Shop at Doune, Perthshire, Scotland. Made all metal Scottish-type flintlock pistols with scroll butt.

**Campbell, William** [about 1740] Made all metal flintlock pistols at Perth, Scotland.

**Capner, Thomas** [about 1810] General gunsmith at Birmingham.

**Cardiffe, Charles** [about 1682] Established a gunsmithery in London.

**Carr** [about 1720] Shop at Lymm, Cheshire. Made flintlock fowling pieces.

**Carr & Cooper** [1800–1820] General gunsmiths in London.

**Carr, George** [about 1865] Custom gunmaker in London.

**Carr, W.** [about 1830] Shop at Lyme Regis, Dorset. General gunsmith.

**Carter, Benjamin** [about 1720] Made flintlock traveling pistols. Shop in London.

**Carter, Edward** [about 1870] Custom gunmaker in London.

**Carter, P.** [about 1780] Made cased flintlock duelling pistols with silver mask butt caps. Shop in London.

**Cartwell, Thomas** [1780–1824] Shop in Doncaster, Yorkshire. Made flintlock pocket pistols and brass barrel blunderbuss type of flintlock coach pistol with top spring bayonet.

Cartwright, Samuel [about 1835] General gunsmith at Bolton, Lancashire.

Carver, Robert [1865–1879] Custom gunmaker in London. His son, Alfred Carver, carried on the business from 1879 to 1893.

Cash, James [about 1800] Shop in Birmingham. General gunsmith.

Caton, William [about 1835] General gunsmith at Preston, Lancashire.

Chamberlain, John [1869–1880] Custom gunmaker in London.

Chamberlain, Thomas [about 1765] Shop in Birmingham. General gunsmith.

Chambers, John [1854–1867] General gunsmith in London.

Champion [about 1830] Shop at Southampton. General gunsmith.

Champion [about 1850] Made percussion sporting guns of fine workmanship at Chichester, Sussex.

Champman, John [about 1815] General gunsmith at Birmingham.

Chance & Son, William [1800–1846] Shops in London and Birmingham. Made four-barrel flintlock pocket pistols with revolving flashpan. Later made percussion naval pistols with belt hook and cased saw-handle percussion duelling pistols.

Chapman [about 1820] General gunsmith at Cranbrook, Kent.

Chapman, Robert [about 1830] Shop at Boston, Lincolnshire. General gunsmith.

Chard [about 1850] Made cased percussion traveling pistols and percussion revolver, Adams Patent, at Croydon, Surrey.

Charters, David [about 1835] General gunsmith at Berwick, Scotland.

B

Chater [about 1790] Shop at Ringwood, Hampshire. General gunsmith.

Chatman [about 1740] Made flintlock fowling pieces in London.

Cherrett, D. [about 1850] Custom gunmaker and importer in London.

Cheshire, William [about 1815] General gunsmith in Birmingham.

Child, William [1820–1850] Shop at 280 Strand, London. Made flintlock pocket pistols of fine workmanship. Later made percussion holster pistols.

Christie, John [1750–1775] Shops at Doune and Stirling, Scotland. Made all metal, steel and silver, flintlock pistols with scroll butt.

Chrystie, James (2 generations) [1766–1820] Made all metal flintlock pistols with scroll butts and ball trigger. Shop in Perth, Scotland.

Churchill, Charles [1869–1892] Custom gunmaker in London. Name changed to E. J. Churchill Ltd. at 32 Orange Street, Leicester Square 1892 to 1900.

Clabrough, J. P. [about 1850] Shop in Lincoln. Made boxlock percussion pocket pistols and pin-fire shotguns.

Clark [about 1800] Made flintlock pocket pistols with under spring bayonet. Shop at Marlow, Buckinghamshire.

Clark [1785–1840] Had Royal Government contract for flintlock muskets. Made double barrel flintlock holster pistols and cannon barrel boxlock flintlock pocket pistols, also flintlock sporting rifles. Shop in Holborn, London. Designed and made a combination flintlock and percussion pistol that could be altered to either form of ignition in the field.

Clark, Charles [1854–1874] Shops in London and Cambridge. Made percussion pocket pistols and cased naval percussion pistols with fittings, also percussion sporting rifles.

**Clarke, C.** [about **1800**] Made cased flintlock traveling pistols in Dublin, Ireland.

**Clarke, D.** [about **1830**] General gunsmith in London.

**Clarke, P.** [**1760–1790**] Shop at 62 Cheapside, London. Made flintlock holster pistols and flintlock musketoons with Royal Cypher. Name changed to R. S. Clarke at 102 Cheapside, 1790 to 1820. Made cased flintlock duelling pistols of fine workmanship.

**Clarkson, I.** [**1680–1730**] Had a Royal Government contract for flintlock muskets and flintlock holster pistols. He also made silver mounted flintlock pocket pistols and cannon barrel Queen Anne–type boxlock flintlock coach pistols of excellent workmanship and design. Made brass barrel blunderbuss type of flintlock pistol for boarding parties of the Royal Navy. Made Ferguson-type breech-loading holster pistols. Shop in London.

**Claude** [**1800–1815**] Shop in London. Made cannon barrel flintlock coach pistols.

**Clayton, A.** [**1860–1880**] Custom gunmaker and dealer in High Street, Southampton. Made cased Tranter Patent double trigger percussion revolvers.

**Clemens** [**1750–1780**] Shop on Piccadilly, London. Made cannon barrel flintlock coach pistols.

**Clement, Charles** [about **1880**] Custom gunmaker in London.

**Clemson** [**1745–1795**] Made cannon barrel boxlock flintlock pocket pistols with folding trigger. Shop at Shrewsbury, Shropshire.

**Clerk, William & James** [about **1630**] Established a gunsmithery in Scotland. Location not known.

**Clive, John** [about **1815**] General gunsmith in Birmingham.

**Clough & Sons, G.** [**1820–1860**] Made cased pairs of percussion traveling pistols and percussion revolvers. Shop at Bath, Somerset.

**Cochrans** [about **1865**] Custom gunmaker in London.

**Coffin, R.** [about **1770**] Shop in London. General gunsmith.

**Cogswell, Benjamin** [**1850–1862**] Custom gunmaker and dealer at 224 Strand, London. Sold cased percussion Tranter Patent revolvers with loading equipment. Name changed to Cogswell & Harrison at same address 1862 to 1880. Became Cogswell & Harrison Co. Ltd. at 168 Piccadilly, London, with plant at 21 Park Road East, Acton, 1880 to 1900.

**Cole** [about **1840**] Shop at Belfast, Ireland. Made cased percussion traveling pistols with all accessories.

**Cole, Elias** [**1720–1775**] Made flintlock blunderbusses with Royal Cypher. Shop in London.

**Cole, John** [**1866–1897**] Custom gunmaker in London.

**Cole, Robert** [**1750–1773**] Shop at Devizes, Wiltshire. Made flintlock pocket pistols.

**Colesby, Ephraim** [about **1860**] Custom gunmaker in London.

**Collett, Joseph** [about **1720**] Shop in London. General gunsmith.

**Collicott, Henry** [**1750–1780**] Made brass barrel flintlock holster pistols. Shop at Bristol, Gloucestershire.

**Collier, Elisha Hayden** [**1812–1852**] Elisha Hayden Collier was an American gunsmith in Boston, Massachusetts, and in 1810 developed a practical flintlock revolving pistol. His model had a revolving cylinder firing through a single barrel. The cylinder was turned by hand after each firing. Unable to interest American capital he went to London in 1811 and was granted a Royal Patent. The piece was 14 inches over-all, had a 6⅜-inch octagonal barrel, smoothbore and .47 caliber. He established a shop at 45 Strand, London. About sixty of the revolving pistols and about twenty-four of the revolving long arms were fabricated. He returned to the United States in 1852 and re-established his gunshop in Boston, Massachusetts, where he was active until his death in 1863.

**Colling, William** [about **1835**] General gunsmith at Hexham, Northumberland.

**Collins** [about **1760**] Shop in Birmingham. General gunsmith.

**Collins, Frederick** [**1840–1860**] Made percussion pocket pistols with spring bayonet. Shop in London.

**Collins, James** [**1800–1854**] Shop at 12 Vigo Lane, Regent Street, London. Made officers' flintlock holster pistols with silver mounts, later three-shot percussion pocket pistol with revolving striker on the hammer, and with folding trigger. Also double barrel, over and under, percussion holster pistols.

**Collis, I.** [about **1800**] Made boxlock flintlock pocket pistols and brass barrel flintlock coach pistols. Also flintlock holster pistols with the Royal Cypher. Shop located in Oxford.

**Collumbell** [**1689–1743**] Shop in London. Made Queen Anne–type boxlock flintlock coach pistols with silver mask butt caps and flintlock holster pistols.

**Colts Patent Repeating Arms, Ltd.** [**1852–1857**] Samuel Colt established his London plant at Besborough Place and Grosvenor Road, Pimlico, Thames Bank, in May 1852, and met with considerable opposition and competition from British gunmakers. He had previously established a depot and retail show room at No. 1 Spring Gardens, Cockspur Street, London. He developed a successful business and received both British and Russian Government contracts. His United States plant and business required his first attention, with its tremendous development and expansion during this period, and he closed out his English operation in 1857. All Colt arms made in England were marked "Col. Sam'l Colt London." Colt arms made at the Hartford, Connecticut, plant for export to the British Empire and Continental Europe were marked "L" after the serial number for the Empire and "E" after the serial number for Europe. All Colt arms sold in England carry the London Proof and View Marks. After Colt closed the London plant he established a sales and show room at 14 Pall Mall, London, from 1857 to 1866 to sell and display his American-made line of arms.

**Conway** [about **1830**] General gunsmith at Poole, Dorsetshire.

**Conway, Thomas** [**1820–1850**] Shop at Manchester. Made cased flintlock traveling pistols and flintlock blunderbusses; later percussion pepperboxes, also double barrel percussion pistols with belt hook, and percussion revolvers, Tranter Patent.

**Conway, W. M.** [about **1840**] General gunsmith at Newcastle under Lyme, Staffordshire.

**Cook** [about **1800**] Made cased flintlock duelling pistols with loading equipment at Dublin, Ireland.

**Cook** [1780–1800] Shop in London. Made officers' flintlock holster pistols.

**Cook** [about 1835] General gunsmith at Lincoln.

**Cook, Benjamin** [about 1805] Shop in Birmingham, general gunsmith.

**Cook & Sons, J. T.** [1850–1870] Custom gunmakers in London.

**Cook, William** [about 1800] Made double barrel flintlock fowling pieces at Perth, Scotland.

**Cook, William and Thomas** (son) [1808–1850] William Cook was a general gunsmith at Bath, Somerset, 1808 to 1832. His son, Thomas, established a gunshop at Shepton Mallet, Somerset, and later at Warminster, Wiltshire, 1832 to 1850.

**Cooke, E.** [about 1718] Established a gunsmithery in London.

**Cookson, John** [1670–1720] Developed a practical and workable repeating flintlock pistol. This operated with a lever on the left side that brought the chamber in line with the barrel. Shop in London.

**Coombs, E.** [1740–1770] Made flintlock fowling pieces at Bath, Somerset.

**Cooper** [about 1790] Shop in London. Made brass barrel, bell muzzle, flintlock swivel boat gun.

**Cooper & Banks** [1822–1860] General gunsmiths in Birmingham. Name changed to **Cooper & Goodman**, 1860 to 1876. Made breech-loading metallic cartridge carbines under Royal Government contract.

**Cooper, George** [about 1835] Shop at Stockton, Durham. General gunsmith.

**Cooper, G. C.** [1880–1893] Custom gunmaker in London.

**Cooper, James Rock** [1840–1853] Shop in Birmingham. Patented a percussion pepperbox in 1843.

**Cork, John** [about 1780] General gunsmith in London.

**Cornforth** [1725–1760] Made cannon barrel boxlock flintlock pocket pistols in London.

**Coutts, William** [1871–1894] Custom gunmaker in London.

**Cowper, T.** [about 1800] Shop at Wrexham, Wales. General gunsmith.

**Cox, Mathew** [about 1840] General gunsmith at Yeovil, Somerset.

**Cox & Son, T.** [about 1860] Made cased percussion revolvers at Southampton.

**Crabb, George** [about 1880] Custom gunmaker in London.

**Cracknell** [1733–1760] Made boxlock, flintlock pocket pistols in London.

**Crane, J. H.** [1868–1879] Shop at 3 Royal Exchange, London. Made cased percussion revolvers, Tranter Patent.

**Cressall, Henry & William** [1856–1873] Custom gunmakers in London.

**Crew** [about 1850] Shop in Tetbury, Gloucestershire. Made cased percussion traveling pistols.

**Crips, H.** [1640–1660] Made brass barrel flintlock blunderbusses in London.

**Crispan, Joseph** [about 1850] Shop at 16 Georges Street, Cork, Ireland. Custom gunmaker.

**Crodler, Thomas** [about 1665] Early flintlock rifle maker in London.

**Crook, Robert** [about 1770] General gunsmith in Birmingham.

**Cross, Daniel** [1800–1812] Shop in Birmingham. General gunsmith.

**Crundwell & Co.** [1835–1850] Made cased pairs of screw barrel percussion traveling pistols with all accessories. Shop in London.

**Cuff, John** [1810–1830] Shop in London. Made double barrel flintlock coach pistols.

**Cullum** [about 1750] Made flintlock holster pistols in London.

**Cumming, William** [1871–1884] Custom gunmaker in London.

**Cutler** [about 1850] Made percussion pepperboxes in Dublin, Ireland.

# NOTES
## C

**Dacot, W.** [about 1835] General gunsmith in London.

**Dafte, John** [1640–1680] Gunsmithery in Shire Lane, London. One of the early London makers to sign his name on a piece. Made flintlock holster pistols.

**Dakin** [about 1840] Made percussion pocket pistols at Nottingham.

**Dalby, David** [about 1835] General gunsmith at Boston, Lincolnshire.

**Dale** [1815–1840] Shop in London and did general gunsmithing. Dale exported about 1000 locks to the United States armory at Springfield, Massachusetts. These were used on the U. S. Army flintlock dragoon pistols, Model 1818, and the name "Dale" was stamped on the inside of the lock plate. These are identified by a gooseneck hammer or cock rare in American arms of that period.

**Dalkin, Thomas** [about 1835] General gunsmith at Barnard Castle, Durham.

**Dalton** [1750–1780] Made flintlock duelling pistols. Shop in Dublin, Ireland.

**Dalton, L.** [about 1830] Shop at Spalding, Lincolnshire. General gunsmith.

**Daniel, James** [1780–1812] Made brass barrel, blunderbuss type of pistol with top spring bayonet. Shop in Birmingham. Name became **Daniel, Cross & Co.** 1812 to 1825.

**Daniell, T.** [1730–1750] Shop at Foster Lane, London. Made four-barrel flintlock pocket pistols.

**Darby, John** [1866–1880] Custom gunmaker in London.

**Daukes, J.** [about 1710] Made flintlock naval pistols with Royal Cypher. Shop in London.

**Davenport, R.** [1800–1820] General gunsmith in Birmingham.

**Davenport, W.** [1690–1720] Made flintlock holster pistols with silver mountings and mask butt plate. Shop in London.

**Davey, W.** [about 1835] General gunsmith at Norwich, Norfolk.

**David & Arnold** [1680–1700] Shop in London. General gunsmiths.

**Davidson, Duncan** [about 1810] General gunsmith in Birmingham.

**Davidson, Joseph** [1790–1820] Shop in London. Made flintlock arms under contract for the East India Company. The proof mark of the company was a heart quartered with the letters V.E.I.C. in each quadrant, starting with V in the upper left-hand quadrant. Under this contract Davidson made single and double barrel flintlock pocket pistols, flintlock holster pistols, and cased pairs of duelling pistols with accessories.

**Davies, T.** [about 1835] General gunsmith in Oswestry, Shropshire.

**Davis** [about 1610] Established a gunsmithery in London.

**Davis, Samson** [1832–1850] Shop at 4 East Smithfield, London. Made a percussion shotgun in which the stock was in two pieces and could be taken apart. Known as a poacher's gun.

**Davis, T.** [1750–1775] Made boxlock flintlock pocket pistols with spring bayonet. Shop in London.

**Davis, W.** [about 1750] Shop in London. Made screw barrel flintlock pocket pistols with detachable daggers like a bayonet.

**Davis, William** [1790–1834] General gunsmith in Birmingham.

**Davison** [about 1820] Shop in Birmingham. General gunsmith.

**Davison, William** [about 1825] Made flintlock pocket pistols. Shop at Alnwick, Northumberland.

**Davy, W.** [1790–1810] Made brass barrel flintlock holster pistols some with extension stock to be used as carbines. Shop in London.

**Daw, George H.** [1780–1840] General gunsmith at 57 Threadneedle Street, London. Name changed to **G. H. Daw & Co.** 1840 to 1849, custom gunmakers and dealers. They made cased double-action percussion revolvers, .44 caliber, with loading accessories. Became **Witton & Daw** 1849 to 1878, and **G. H. Daw & Son** 1878 to 1889, then the **Daw Gun Company** 1889 to 1892.

**Dawes** [1780–1800] Made flintlock holster pistols and double barrel flintlock fowling pieces. Shop in London.

**Dawes, William & Samuel** [1798–1812] General gunsmiths in Birmingham.

**Dawkes, John** [1767–1780] Shop in Birmingham. General gunsmith.

**Dawse** [about 1780] General gunsmith. Shop in Maidstone, Kent.

**Dawstin, William** [about 1630] One of seven London gunsmiths whose name appeared in the text of a Commission granted by Charles I, to make Royal arms.

**Day, E. C. W.** [1810–1830] Made double barrel boxlock flintlock pocket pistols at Derby.

**Day, Frank** [1778–1810] General gunsmith in London.

**Daykin, F.** [about 1780] Made boxlock flintlock pocket pistols and screw barrel flintlock holster pistols at Nottingham.

**Deacon, S.** [about 1835] General gunsmith. Shop at Monmouth.

**Deacon, Thomas** [about 1830] Shop at Stafford. General gunsmith.

**Deakin, F.** [about 1815] Made flintlock rifles at Birmingham.

**Dealtry** [about 1725] Made brass cannon barrel flintlock coach pistols with mask butt cap. Shop in London.

**Deane, Adams & Deane** [1851–1856] John Deane, Robert and John Adams (brothers), were owners of this firm who manufactured the Adams Patent percussion revolver. There were three models; the Dragoon .50 caliber barrel 7½ or 8 inches, the Navy .44 caliber barrel 5¾ or 6¼ inches, and the Pocket Model .32 caliber barrel 4½ inches. They were located at 30 King William Street, London. Deane, Adams & Deane were dissolved in 1856 and **John Deane & Son** established a shop at London Bridge Street, London. John Deane took over the percussion revolver patents of William Harding, issued in March 1858. This percussion revolver was called the Deane-Harding revolver. The arm was double action and solid frame, .44 caliber and .32 caliber. The patent was in the lock mechanism and after Royal Ordnance tests was considered too complicated for the Services, although it was popular with the officers in the British and Indian Armies. Deane also made percussion carbines under Royal Government contract and percussion pepperboxes and a small caliber cased percussion pistol known as a ladies' "muff" pistol.

**Deane, George** [about 1750] Made officers' flintlock holster pistols of fine workmanship. Shop at Fish Street Hill, London.

**Dee, Theodore** [about 1750] General gunsmith at Birmingham.

**Delaney** [1780–1800] Shop in Dublin, Ireland. General gunsmith.

**Delany, H.** [1690–1750] Made officers' flintlock holster pistols of fine workmanship. He made also brass barrel flintlock blunderbusses and flintlock rifled carbines. One of his outstanding works was a silver mounted flintlock fowling piece of excellent design and balance. Shop located in London.

**Dempsey** [about 1780] Made brass mounted flintlock coach pistols. Shop at Dublin, Ireland.

**Dennison, John** [about 1718] Established a gunsmithery in London.

**Denry** [about 1860] Custom gunmaker in Liverpool.

**Dent, Thomas** [about 1835] Shop at Stokesley, Yorkshire. General gunsmith.

**Denyer, B** [1780–1800] Made cased flintlock duelling pistols with all accessories. Shop at 66 St. Mary's Street, Portsmouth, Hampshire.

**Denyer, Bernard** [1850–1875] Custom gunsmith in London.

**Dermott** [about 1790] General gunsmith in Dublin, Ireland.

**Devillers, N.** [1750–1780] Made cannon barrel flintlock coach pistols. Shop in London.

**Dick, W.** [about 1750] Shop in London. Made flintlock muskets with Royal Cypher.

**Dickenson** [about 1840] Made double barrel percussion sporting guns in London.

**Dickinson, Herbert** [1854–1880] Made double barrel pin-fire shotguns with patented breech-opening action. Shop in London.

**Dickson & Son, John** [1820–1850] Shop at 63 Princess Street, Edinburgh, Scotland. Made cased double barrel,

over and under, percussion traveling pistols, with all accessories, and double barrel percussion sporting rifles.

**Diemar, E. M.** [about 1750] General gunsmith in London. Made flintlock duelling pistols.

**Dixson, Samuel** [1800–1832] Shop at Leicester. Made screw barrel boxlock flintlock pocket pistols.

**Dobson, John** [about 1770] General gunsmith in Dublin, Ireland.

**Dobson, T.** [about 1780] Made flintlock coach pistols with silver mountings. Shop in London.

**Dobson & Baker** [about 1800] Shop in London. Made blunderbuss-type flintlock coach pistol with top spring bayonet.

**Docker, Thomas** [about 1770] General gunsmith in Birmingham.

**Docker, W.** [1750–1790] Shop in Derby. Made double barrel, over and under, flintlock pocket pistols.

**Dodson, E.** [about 1850] Made cased percussion sea captains' pistols. Shop in Louth, Ireland.

**Dolep** [1720–1760] General gunsmith in London.

**Donald, Atkey & Co.** [1872–1885] Custom gunmakers in London.

**Dooley, W.** [1840–1872] Shop at 11 Ranelagh Street, Liverpool. Made percussion pepperboxes, cased percussion traveling pistols and cased percussion duelling pistols, with loading equipment, also made percussion revolvers of Kerr Patent.

**Doubleday, T.** [1800–1835] General gunsmith at Newark upon Trent, Nottinghamshire.

**Dougall, James D.** [1864–1887] Shops at London and Glasgow, Scotland. Made cased percussion traveling pistols and double barrel percussion sporting guns. Name changed to **James D. Dougall & Sons** 1887 to 1893.

**Dowling** [about **1850**] Shop in Dublin, Ireland. Made percussion pepperboxes and double barrel percussion sporting guns.

**Dowling, Frederick** [**1865–1877**] Made double barrel percussion naval pistols. Shop in London.

**Draper, William** [**1780–1800**] Shop at Maldon, Essex. Made brass barrel flintlock blunderbusses with top spring bayonet.

**Dresse, Laloux Co.** [about **1880**] Custom gunmakers and importers in London.

**Drew, John** [about **1715**] Made screw barrel Queen Anne–type flintlock coach pistols with silver lion mask butt cap.

**Drisket & Co., A.** [**1866–1878**] Custom gunmakers in London.

**Drissen, Fred** [about **1875**] Shop in London. General gunsmith.

**Drury** [**1775–1790**] General gunsmith in Liverpool. Name changed to **Drury & Son** 1790 to 1810.

**Dubois** [**1720–1750**] Made flintlock blunderbusses with Royal Cypher. Shop in London.

**Dugard, R.** [about **1840**] Shop in Birmingham. Made double barrel percussion pocket pistols.

**Dunbar, David** [about **1790**] Made all metal steel flintlock pistols with scroll butts. Shop in Edinburgh, Scotland.

**Dunderdale, Mabson & Co.** [**1780–1813**] Shop in Birmingham. Made screw barrel boxlock flintlock pocket pistols with folding trigger. Name changed to **Dunderdale, Mabson & Labron,** 1813 to 1832. Made flintlock fowling pieces and brass barrel flintlock blunderbusses with top spring bayonet. Name again changed to **Dunderdale & Company** 1832 to 1850.

**Dunn, Jeffery** [**1730–1760**] General gunsmith in London.

**Dunn, John & Joseph** [about **1770**] Shop in Birmingham. General gunsmiths.

**Dupe, W. W.** [**1770–1813**] Made cased pairs of flintlock duelling pistols with loading equipment. Shop in Oxford.

**Dust, John** [**1790–1830**] Shop in London. Made double barrel flintlock pocket pistols.

**Dutton, Daniel** [about **1800**] General gunsmith in Birmingham.

**Dutton, John** [**1790–1820**] Made screw barrel flintlock pocket pistols and brass barrel flintlock holster pistols. Shop in London.

**Dyball, Edward** [about **1860**] Custom gunmaker in London.

**Dyer, Richard** [about **1715**] Shop in London. General gunsmith.

# NOTES
## D

**Eadon, T.** [1800–1840] Shop at Lancaster, Lancashire. Made flintlock holster pistols and later percussion naval pistols with belt hook.

**East & Co., Edward** [about 1870] Custom gunmakers in London.

**Eaton & Co., William** [about 1875] Shop in East London. Made pin-fire sporting shotguns.

**Ebbutt** [1660–1714] General gunsmith in London.

**Ebrail** [about 1840] Shop located in Shropshire. General gunsmith.

**Edens, Nathaniel** [about 1650] Established a gunsmithery in London.

**Edge, John William** [1830–1845] Made percussion pocket pistols with folding trigger, and double barrel, side-by-side, percussion pistols with belt hook. Shop in Manchester.

**Edge, R.** [1725–1761] Made cannon barrel boxlock flintlock coach pistols with silver mask butt caps also made flintlock muskets and flintlock holster pistols with Royal Cypher. Shop in London.

**Edgson** [1810–1830] Shop at Stamford, Lincolnshire. Made screw barrel boxlock flintlock pocket pistols with folding trigger.

**Edwards** [about 1780] Made cased flintlock duelling pistols with gold mounting of fine design and workmanship. Shop in Dublin, Ireland.

**Edwards, Francis** [about 1765] General gunsmith in Birmingham.

**Edwards, W.** [1770–1820] Shop at Devonport, Devonshire. Made cased flintlock coach and also holster pistols.

**Egan, Samuel G.** [1860–1893] Made boxlock, percussion pocket pistols. Shop in London.

**Egg, Charles** [about 1850] Made percussion pepperboxes also percussion military muskets under Royal Government contract. Shop in London.

**Egg, Durs** [1770–1834] Durs Egg, a celebrated London gunsmith, had the Royal Warrant of the Prince Regent, later George IV. He had a number of Royal Government contracts for flintlock muskets, rifles, and carbines. Probably made all of the military Ferguson flintlock breech-loading rifles and made a flintlock breech-loading carbine of his own design. Durs Egg was one of the early makers of, over and under, double barrel pistols and made a number of flintlock holster pistols of this type. His shop for civilian arms was at 1 Pall Mall, London. The name was changed to **D. I. Egg** (probably a son or nephew) 1834 to 1865.

**Egg, Henry, Sr.** [1810–1851] General gunsmith in London. His son Henry, Jr., carried on the business from 1851 to 1869 and Henry, Jr's. sons, Henry III, and William, carried on from 1869 to 1880. The latter made double barrel pin-fire sporting shotguns.

**Egg, Joseph H.** [1820–1860] Shop on Piccadilly, London. Made percussion holster pistols with swivel ramrod and percussion revolvers, Tranter Patent.

**Eginton, John** [about 1800] General gunsmith in Birmingham.

**Ellis, Henry** [1750–1780] Shop at Doncaster, Yorkshire. Made flintlock coach pistols with silver mask butt caps.

**Ellis, Thomas B.** [1822–1835] General gunsmith in Birmingham.

**Ellis, W.** [about 1840] Made cased pairs of percussion traveling pistols. Shop in London.

**Elsley** [about 1750] Shop in London. Made cased flintlock duelling pistols with loading equipment.

**Elvins, Amos** [about **1870**] Custom gunmaker in London.

**Elwell, Henry** [**1810–1850**] Made flintlock holster pistols and later percussion pistols with belt hook. Shop in London.

**Emme, John** [**1860–1875**] Custom gunmaker in London.

**Emms, W.** [about **1780**] Shop in Birmingham. General gunsmith.

**Enfield Royal Manufactory** (Royal Armoury) [**1855** to date] Prior to 1811 all Royal arms were made under Government contract and in this year the Royal Government established a Royal armory at Enfield, 11 miles north of London. It is interesting to note that the British Government had no official state-maintained arms factory. Until this date all government arms were made under given specifications with private contractors. The French Government on the other hand established in 1718 their own "Manufactures Royales" at Charleville, Saint-Etienne, and Maubeuge. After the battle of Waterloo in 1815 the House of Commons gradually withdrew all appropriations from Enfield and it was used as a depot. No arms were made there. After the beginning of the Crimean War the Birmingham gunmakers struck for higher wages and the Royal Government's decision was to re-establish Enfield as a manufacturing armory. General Raglan, then Master-General of Ordnance, strongly urged this move. The work of extending the buildings at Enfield was completed in February 1855, and in midyear production was started. The first model of the Enfield percussion rifle weighed 9 lbs. 3 oz., caliber .577 and barrel length 3 feet 3 inches. Between 1857 and 1861 certain patterns of breech-loading carbines were supplied to the cavalry for experimental field tests to consider their use to the Services. In 1866 the Board of Ordnance approved the Jacob Snider Patent for breech-loading arms. With the breech loading a special cartridge was invented by Colonel Boxer. In 1871 the Martini–Henry magazine action was adapted, .45 caliber.

**Enty, John** [**1825–1837**] General gunsmith in London.

**Eplett, Joseph** [about **1830**] Shop on High Street, Taunton, Somerset. General gunsmith.

**Erskine & Co., James** [about **1870**] Custom gunmakers and importers in London.

**Essex** [about **1750**] Made flintlock duelling pistols in London.

**Evans** [**1800–1820**] Shop in Cambridge. General gunsmith.

**Evans** [**1700–1725**] Made brass barrel flintlock blunderbuss type of pistol. Shop in Dublin, Ireland.

**Evans, James & John** [about **1810**] Shop in Carmarthen, Wales. Made double barrel flintlock fowling pieces.

**Evans, Meredith** [about **1815**] General gunsmith in Birmingham.

**Evans, Robert** [about **1840**] Made boxlock percussion pocket pistols. Shop in Birmingham.

**Evans, William** [**1883–1900**] Custom gunmaker and dealer at 67 St. James Street, London.

**Everard, William** [about **1715**] General gunsmith in London.

**Ewen** [about **1775**] Made double barrel flintlock fowling pieces in Edinburgh, Scotland.

# NOTES
E

**Fairfax, William Henry** [about 1855] Made percussion revolver, Webley Patent. Shop in Birmingham.

**Fairman, James** [1850–1868] Shop in London. Made double barrel percussion sporting guns.

**Farlow, R.** [1702–1750] Made brass barrel flintlock blunderbusses with Royal Cypher. Shop in London.

**Farmer, G.** [1720–1750] Shop in Cardiff, Wales. Made flintlock pocket pistols and cased flintlock duelling pistols.

**Farmer, Joseph** [1718–1762] Made double barrel boxlock flintlock pocket pistols. Also had Royal Government contracts for flintlock muskets of the Militia pattern of 1745 and flintlock muskets of the Grenadiers' pattern. Shop in London.

**Farnum** [about 1745] General gunsmith in London.

**Farquharson, John** [1871–1889] Born in 1833 at Moulin, Perthshire. He was a gamekeeper or "gillie" and a famous marksman. Won the championship of Scotland in 1863. In 1871 established a gunsmithery near Blairgowrie in Perthshire. In May 1872, patented a hammerless, falling block action, breech-loading metallic cartridge rifle. The action had a long latched lever which produced good leverage for extraction of the shell and was an improvement over the falling block actions up to that time. In 1889 he retired from gunmaking and died at Dunay, Perthshire in 1893.

**Fell, John** [about 1835] General gunsmith in Lancaster, Lancashire.

**Felstead, Thomas William** [about 1855] Shop in London. General gunsmith.

**Fenton, R.** [1780–1830] Shop in London. Made cased flintlock coach pistols and double barrel flintlock fowling pieces. Later percussion dragoon pistols with swivel ramrod and saw-handle percussion duelling pistols.

**Ferguson, Patrick** [1774–1780] Born 1744 at Pitfour, Scotland. Entered the army 1765 as an officer in the Royal North British Dragoons and saw service in the West Indies prior to the War of Independence. On June 1, 1776, Major Patrick Ferguson demonstrated at Woolwich, England, before a commission of the Master-General of Ordnance his flintlock breech-loading rifle. Major Ferguson described it as "a rifle gun on a new construction which will astonish all beholders." The rifle had a perpendicular breech plug equipped with a screw device so as to make it possible to lower it by one revolution of the trigger guard which served as the handle. When the breech plug was lowered, an opening was left in the top of the barrel at the breech. A spherical bullet was dropped into this opening with the muzzle of the piece held downward and rolled forward through the chamber where it was stopped by the lands of the rifling. A charge of powder was then poured into the opening, filling the chamber behind the bullet. One revolution of the trigger guard closed the breech and the rifle was ready for priming and firing. Major Ferguson demonstrated that six aimed shots per minute could be fired with an accuracy creditable to any rifle of that period. Advancing riflemen could fire four aimed shots per minute; reloading being possible while the soldier was running. Another advantage of the Ferguson rifle was that it could be loaded while the soldier was in a prone position. On December 2, 1776, Major Ferguson was given a Royal Patent (# 1139) for his breechloader, and the arm became the first breechloader used by organized troops in any country. About 200 Ferguson rifles were made under Royal Government contract by Durs Egg and Ezekiel Baker, and used to equip Major Ferguson's 2nd Battalion, 71st Regiment, Light Infantry Highlanders. His riflemen, under his command, saw action on September 11, 1777, at the Battle of Brandywine and, later, at Stony Point, New York, and Little Egg Harbor, New Jersey. He was with Sir Henry Clinton's expedition against Charleston, South Carolina, and moved northward after the capture of Charleston, through the Carolinas to join Cornwallis. It is doubtful that more than a hundred of Ferguson's rifles were used in the Battle of Kings Mountain, North Carolina, October 7, 1780, when Lieutenant Colonel Ferguson was killed.

The Ferguson Patent sporting rifles were made by S. Turner, and Wilson of London, by Newton of Grantham, and F. Innis of Edinburgh, Scotland.

**Field & Co., Alfred [1890–1900]** Custom gunmakers in London.

**Field, John P. [1840–1866]** Made percussion holster pistols at Birmingham.

**Field, I.** [about **1780**] Shop at Tower Hill, London. Made flintlock holster pistols.

**Field, T. W. [1750–1790]** Shop at Aylesbury, Buckinghamshire. Made screw brass barrel flintlock pocket pistols.

**Fisher [1810–1825]** Made brass barrel flintlock holster pistols and brass barrel flintlock naval pistols with belt hook. Shop at Bristol.

**Fisher, Charles B. [1790–1826]** Made flintlock pocket and coach pistols. He also made brass barrel flintlock blunderbusses and large bore flintlock shotguns used for commercial duck hunting. Shop in London.

**Fisher, George [1670–1695]** Made flintlock carbines with Royal Cypher. Shop in London.

**Fisher, Timothy** [about **1830**] General gunsmith in Ormskirk, Lancashire.

**Fisher, William [1850–1867]** Shop in London. Made boxlock percussion pocket pistols with folding trigger.

**Fisherden** [about **1830**] General gunsmith in Tonbridge, Kent.

**Fitzchoice** [about **1780**] General gunsmith in London.

**Fletcher, E. [1700–1720]** Shop in London. General gunsmith.

**Fletcher, Gervas** [about **1720**] General gunsmith in Stanford, Essex.

**Fletcher, Thomas [1835–1855]** Shop in Gloucester. Made percussion pepperboxes and percussion revolvers, Adams Patent.

**Fletcher, Thomas [1866–1872]** Custom gunmaker in London.

**Fletcher, W.** [about **1830**] Shop in Tewkesbury, Gloucestershire. Made flintlock fowling pieces.

**Flewitt, John** [about **1800**] General gunsmith in Birmingham.

**Fliegenschmidt, Max** [about **1880**] Custom gunmaker in London.

**Flong** [about **1750**] Shop in London. Made naval boarding flintlock pistols with brass mountings and Royal Cypher.

**Flood & Co.** [about **1815**] Made flintlock fowling pieces in London.

**Foad** [about **1690**] Established a gun barrel making shop on Tewen Street, London.

**Forbes** [about **1810**] General gunsmith in Liverpool.

**Forbes, Alexander [1685–1750]** Made all metal steel flintlock pistols with ramshorn butt. Shop at Elgin, Scotland.

**Ford, J.** [1810–1820] Shop in London. General gunsmith.

**Ford, Richard** [1860–1868] Custom gunmaker in London.

**Forrest** [about 1800] Made cased silver mounted flintlock duelling pistols with loading equipment. Shop in Oxford.

**Forsyth, Alexander John** [1805–1819] The Reverend Alexander John Forsyth, inventor of the percussion method of the ignition of gunpowder, was born at the Manse of Belhelvie, Aberdeenshire, Scotland, eight miles north of Aberdeen, December 28, 1768, the son of Reverend James Forsyth, minister of Belhelvie and Isabella, daughter of Reverend Walter Syme, minister of Tullynessle. He entered Kings College, Aberdeen, in 1782 and graduated as Master of Arts 1786. Having decided to study for the Church, he attended divinity classes and was licensed for the Ministry, October 13, 1790. On December 1, 1790, his father died and the Parish petitioned that his son should succeed him. On August 24, 1791, he received the Presentation of the Crown and became the Minister of the Parish which he held for 52 years until his death.

Much of his leisure time was spent on chemistry and mechanics, in a little garden house on the Manse property which was known by the local people as the "Minister's Smiddy." Years before when shooting wild fowl on a loch near the Manse he had first thought of an improvement of the flintlock fowling piece for overcoming its disadvantages. He constructed a sighted hood over the flintlock which developed later into the percussion lock. He was known to say in later years "that his invention of the percussion lock was the result of enjoying his leisure hours

amusing himself with scientific study."

Dr. Forsyth made his first successful percussion lock in 1805 after years of experiment with detonating mixtures and devices to fire, and he shot with this fowling piece through the season of that year. In the spring of 1806 he took his models to London and among other sporting friends showed them to Sir Joseph Banks, who showed them to the Master-General of Ordnance, Francis Rawdon-Hastings (Lord Moira). Lord Moira sent for Dr. Forsyth and asked him to make some further experiments at the Tower of London. The tests and experiments of the lock were successful, and Lord Moira insisted that Forsyth stay and make further tests; the Master-General of Ordnance obtained for Forsyth a leave of absence from the Aberdeen Presbytery. Dr. Forsyth now applied himself to the task before him to construct a lock that would ignite a charge of gunpowder with certainty, which could be easily primed, and which should be secured against damp and accidental discharge. To accomplish this required a very different construction of the percussion part of the lock from that which was required when ignition alone was the object, and he found that making plausible sketches on paper answered no good purpose until their effects were ascertained by operating parts made of steel.

After overcoming many unforeseen prejudices of London workmen, who neither knew nor understood the nature of the work on which they were employed, Dr. Forsyth had still another obstacle in his way. Hitherto, for several reasons, he had preferred detonating mercury for a priming powder, as it was cleaner than any of the other detonating powders then made. But now when all parts of the percussion lock were required to be made with great accuracy, if they were to produce the desired effect, it was found that detonating mercury could not always be made with the same degree of strength. Also, that even when weakest, it always burst or swelled that part of the lock which contained it when inflamed, and that other kinds of detonating powder then in use were too foul. Dr. Forsyth, therefore, had to compound a new detonating priming powder which answered his purpose, but this was attended with considerable danger. Compounding and experimenting with these powders were not then well understood by chemists of whom several had been burned by explosions. They refused to make any quantity for him, and thus Dr. Forsyth was under the necessity of compounding them himself.

These various difficulties being at last overcome, Dr. Forsyth developed a lock, the principle of which was approved by the Master-General of Ordnance in April 1807. These locks were tested on a carbine and a 3-pound cannon and were fairly successful. At this time John Pitt, Earl of Chatham, was appointed Master-General of Ordnance succeeding Lord Moira, and he was of the opinion that prevailed in the Army at that time that the flintlock should not be changed. Dr. Forsyth was ordered to clean out "his rubbish" and leave the Tower. After his removal from the Tower, he took out a patent on his invention (No. 3032 Crown Patents) dated July 4, 1807, and stated in his patent specifications "instead of permitting the touch-hole or vent of the pieces of artillery, firearms, etc., to communicate with the open air and instead of giving fire by lighted match or flint and steel or by other matter in a state of actual combustion applied to a priming in an open pan, I do so close the touch-hole or vent by means of a plug or sliding piece so as to exclude the open air and to prevent any sensible escape of the blast or explosive gas or vapour outwards or from the

priming of the charge and as much as it is possible to force the said priming to go in the direction of the charge and to set fire to the same and not to be wasted in the open air." The celebrated James Watt assisted him in drawing up these patent specifications, and Watt at that time described the invention as "an advantageous method of discharging or giving fire to artillery and all other firearms, mines, chambers, cavities and places in which gunpowder or other combustible matter is or may be put to the purpose of explosion."

The principle of the patent was that the container pivoted under the hammer, was divided in half—the lower portion being filled with the detonating powder closed with a ball valve. On turning this through 180 degrees a small amount of the powder was dropped into the other half which was then turned back to normal position. This was the amount for the priming charge. A spring pin was then struck by the hammer of the piece and the charge fired through the vent into the chamber. The container also acted as a magazine of priming powder and held about twenty charges.

Dr. Forsyth in 1808 set up a gunshop at 10 Piccadilly, London, under the name of **Forsyth & Company,** and to assist him in the business as a practical gunsmith secured the services of James Purdey, formerly with Joseph Manton. Dr. Forsyth was actively interested in the business until 1819, when the Company moved to 8 Leicester Street, Leicester Square and closed in 1826.

An advertisement of Forsyth & Company reads: "The Forsyth patent gunlock is entirely different from the common gunlock. It produces inflammation by means of percussion and supersedes the use of flints. Its principle advantages are the following: The rapid and complete inflammation of the whole charge of gunpowder in the chamber of the barrel. The prevention of the loss of force through the touch-hole. Perfect security against rain or damp in the priming. No flash from the pan and less risk of accidental discharge of the piece than when the common lock is used. The charge of gunpowder to be from one third to one fourth less than when the flintlock is used."

A number of the keenest sportsmen of the day endorsed Dr. Forsyth's Patent lock, among them Colonel Hawker, sportsman and author, who had been a die-hard on the flintlock, and on February 1, 1814, H. Baring, M.P., an ardent sportsman wrote Dr. Forsyth from Somerley House: "I think I may now congratulate you on having made your Patent lock perfect and I venture to predict that in a few years nothing else will be used by sportsmen in this country. I have shot with your guns for the last four years entirely, and under their different stages of improvement, and few persons can be better qualified than myself to form a practical opinion of them. I shoot every day it is possible to go out from the beginning of the season to the end and I am often in the predicament of firing my gun as often as my barrels will bear to be fired in one day."

Rev. Dr. Forsyth's principle of ignition by percussion or blow of the hammer attracted the attention of gunsmiths all over the world. First an iron cap was used, then pewter caps: Joseph Manton, London; Durs Egg, London; and Joshua Shaw, Philadelphia, Pennsylvania, claimed the present copper percussion cap; but there is good evidence that Shaw made the first copper cap in Philadelphia in 1816, and by 1830 the copper cap and nipple were recognized by the gun trade on both continents.

However, the Ordnance Department of the British Army was slow to act on the new system and the Duke of Wellington has been charged with too great an affection for "Brown Bess" as the army flintlock musket was familiarly called. At last official repugnance gave way, and in 1834 Forsyth's invention was tested at Woolwich Arsenal, 6000 rounds from 6 flintlocks and 6000 rounds from 6 percussion muskets were fired in all weathers with the result that the superiority of the percussion system was completely established. Their range was more accurate and more rapid fire was attained, the recoil less, fewer misfires and a great saving in ammunition. In 1836 the first percussion muskets were issued to troops, and the 3rd Grenadier and the 1st Coldstream Guard Regiments were the first to receive them. It is interesting to note that the first percussion musket used in the field was during the First China War at the battle of Amoy, August 26, 1841, by the 55th Border Regiment, second battalion, who changed from flint to percussion muskets at Calcutta.

Dr. Forsyth had received £100 from Lord Moira for expenses; but no remuneration for himself. On February 2, 1840 Mr. Alexander Bannerman, M.P. for Aberdeen, petitioned the House of Commons and Lord Brougham then head of the Honourable Board of Ordnance for recognition of Dr. Forsyth's services.

On April 21, 1842, the Lords of the Treasury on recommendation of the Master-General of Ordnance granted £200 to Dr. Forsyth "for remuneration as the original inventor of percussion firearms."

Dr. Forsyth never married and on June 11, 1843, died at the Manse in Belhelvie and is buried in the churchyard there. Some four months after his death the Master-General and the Board of Ordnance considered the former remuneration inadequate and on reconsideration awarded £1,000 divided among the three surviving relatives. Dr. Forsyth had patriotically refused an offer from the French Government for £20,000 for his invention.

On January 30, 1930, a tablet erected by public subscription to The Reverend Alexander John Forsyth was unveiled in the Tower of London by Lord Cottesloe, Chairman of the National Rifle Association. He said on this occasion: "Forsyth was the only man in the world in whose honor a salute was fired every day in the year. The sportsman with his gun, the soldier at the rifle range or in battle and the gunner at the canon, all unconsciously pay a tribute to the modest but courageous Scottish Minister who invented the percussion lock."

**Fort, T.** [1702–1714] Made brass mounted flintlock holster pistols with Royal Cypher. Shop in London.

**Forth** [1800–1813] Made brass barrel flintlock coach blunderbusses. Shop at York.

**Forth, W.** [about 1830] General gunsmith at Beverley, Yorkshire.

**Foster, Charles** [about 1800] Shop in Birmingham. General gunsmith.

**Foster, Joseph** [about 1835] General gunsmith at Hexham, Northumberland.

**Foster, Rowland** [about 1630] Established a gunsmithery in London.

**Foster & Woodward** [about 1835] General gunsmiths at Doncaster, Yorkshire.

**Fotherby, Christopher** [1800–1820] Made steel barrel flintlock blunderbusses. Shop at Leeds, Yorkshire.

**Fotherby, E.** [about 1830] Shop at Wakefield, Yorkshire. General gunsmith.

**Fowler, Thomas** [1790–1830] Made cased gold mounted flintlock duelling pistols with loading equipment, also brass barrel flintlock blunderbusses with top spring bayonet. Shop in Dublin, Ireland.

**Francis** [about 1780] General gunsmith in London.

**Franck, Ernest Frederick** [about 1875] Custom gunmaker in London.

**Francotte, Auguste** [1877–1893] Importer and custom gunmaker in London.

**Fraser, D. & J.** [about 1870] Shop at 4 Leith Street, Edinburgh, Scotland. Made cased double barrel, over and under, "express" metallic cartridge rifles. These were for big-game hunting and the case carried all cleaning accessories.

**Fraser, John** [about 1705] Shop at Inverness, Scotland. Made flintlock heavy wall guns.

**Fray, T.** [about 1835] General gunsmith at Leicester.

**Freeman, Isaac** [1683–1725] Made cannon barrel, blunderbuss-type flintlock pistols. Shop in London.

**Freeman, James** (2 generations) [1705–1782] Famous gunsmiths in London. A number of their pieces still in existence. Made Queen Anne–type boxlock flintlock pocket pistols with silver mask butt caps (hallmark 1705), flintlock coach pistols with silver mountings (hallmark 1782). Also made brass barrel flintlock holster pistols and flintlock muskets, both with Royal Cypher.

**Freeth, Charles** [1748–1760] Made flintlock holster pistols with Royal Cypher. Shop in London.

**Frere, Thomas** [about 1655] Established a gunsmithery in London. Made flintlock pistols, carbines and blunderbusses under a Royal Commission.

**Frost** [about **1780**] General gunsmith at Peterborough, Northampton.

**Fuller, George** [**1850–1880**] Shop at 280 Strand, London. Had Royal Warrant. Made percussion sporting guns.

**Fullerd, W.** [about **1735**] General gunsmith in London.

**Furber, I.** [about **1785**] Made double barrel, over and under, flintlock pocket pistols with silver mask butt cap. Shop in Birmingham.

**Furlong, Nicholas** [about **1855**] Custom gunmaker in London.

**Furness, E.** [**1819–1832**] Shop at Huddersfield, Yorkshire. General gunsmith.

# NOTES

## F

**Gabitas** [about **1775**] General gunsmith at Bristol.

**Gallyon & Sons, William** [**1784–1840**] Shop at Cambridge. General gunsmiths.

**Galton, Samuel** [**1790–1812**] Shops at London and Birmingham. Under Royal Government contract, made flintlock holster pistols and flintlock muskets.

**Galton, Thomas** [**1750–1795**] Had Royal Government contract for flintlock holster pistols and flintlock carbines, also made flintlock naval officers' pistols with belt hook and silver mountings. Shops in London and Birmingham.

**Gamble, William** [**1800–1830**] Shop at Wisbeck, Cambridgeshire. Made three-barrel flintlock pocket pistols.

**Gameson & Co.** [**1800–1860**] Made flintlock coach pistols and pairs of saw-handle flintlock duelling pistols. Later made cased percussion duelling pistols. Shop in London.

**Gandon, Philip** [**1750–1770**] General gunsmith in London.

**Garden, Robert** (2 generations) [**1789–1830**] Shop at 29 Piccadilly, London. Under Royal Government contract made flintlock holster pistols and flintlock carbines.

**Gardner, James** [about **1765**] General gunsmith at Birmingham.

**Gardner, John** [**1813–1834**] Made flintlock pocket pistols. Shop at Newcastle upon Tyne, Northumberland.

**Gardner, W. T.** [about **1850**] General gunsmith in London.

**Gass, D.** [about **1860**] Custom gunmaker at 42 Oxford Street, London.

**Gastrell** [**1675–1720**] Shop in London. General gunsmith.

**Gatehouse** [**1750–1800**] Shops at London and Portsmouth, Southampton. Made boxlock flintlock pocket pistols and officers' flintlock naval pistols of fine workmanship.

**George** [about **1800**] Shop at Worcester. Made flintlock "duck foot" pistol with the four barrels spread like the four fingers of the hand, one lock and hammer and the four barrels fired at one time. Also made brass barrel flintlock blunderbusses.

**Gibbs, George** [**1845–1870**] Shop at 29 Corn Street, Bristol. Made percussion pepperboxes and percussion sporting guns.

**Gibbons** [about **1785**] Made brass barrel flintlock holster pistols with Royal Cypher. Shop at Birmingham.

**Gibson, Joseph** [about **1835**] Shop at Stockton, Durham. General gunsmith.

**Gibson, T.** [about **1750**] General gunsmith on Lombard Street, London.

**Gilbert** [about **1850**] Made cased percussion traveling pistols with all accessories. Shop in London.

**Gilks, Charles H.** [**1857–1864**] General gunsmith in London. Name changed to **Gilks, Wilson & Co.** of both London and Birmingham 1864 to 1869. Had Royal Government contract for percussion carbines. Name again changed to **C. H. Gilks & Co.** 1869 to 1890. Had Royal Government contract for percussion military rifles.

**Gill, John** [**1750–1770**] Shops in London and Birmingham. Made boxlock flintlock pocket pistols and double barrel flintlock holster pistols. Name changed to **Gill & Parkes** from 1770 to 1808. Had Royal Government contract for flintlock muskets.

**Gill, Robert** [**1800–1832**] Shop at Richmond, Surrey. Made cased flintlock duelling pistols with loading equipment.

**Gill, Thomas** [1770–1812] Made screw barrel flintlock pocket pistols and double barrel flintlock coach pistols with under spring bayonet. Also made double barrel flintlock fowling pieces. Shop in London.

**Gillette** [1790–1830] Made flintlock pocket and coach pistols. Shop in Bristol.

**Gills** [1780–1800] Made boxlock flintlock pocket pistols in London.

**Glass, I.** [1720–1779] Shop in London. Made cannon barrel flintlock pocket pistols and Cookson type of repeating flintlock pistol.

**Glass, Thomas** [about 1830] General gunsmith at Bridgnorth, Shropshire.

**Glaysner, John** [about 1865] Custom gunmaker in London.

**Glukman** [about 1860] Had Royal Government contract for percussion muskets. Shop in Birmingham.

**Goddard** [about 1775] Shop at Salisbury, Wiltshire. Made cannon barrel flintlock pocket pistols.

**Goddard** [about 1850] General gunsmith in Birmingham.

**Godsall** [about 1800] Made cannon barrel flintlock coach pistols with silver mask butt cap. Shop in Gloucester.

**Godsell** [about 1740] General gunsmith in London.

**Godsell, H.** [about 1830] Shop in Hertford. General gunsmith.

**Goff, Daniel** [1779–1810] Made arms under contract for the East India Company. Made screw barrel boxlock flintlock pocket pistols with folding trigger; flintlock holster pistols; and heavy flintlock wall pivot gun. Located in London.

**Goff, Samuel F.** [1879–1889] Custom gunmaker in London.

**Golden, William** [1834–1851] Shop at Huddersfield, Yorkshire. Made double barrel, over and under, percussion pocket pistols.

**Golding, William** [1770–1820] Shops at London and St. Edmunds, Suffolk. Made screw barrel flintlock coach pistols and brass barrel flintlock blunderbusses with top spring bayonet.

**Goldsworthy, Thomas** [1800–1839] Made boxlock flintlock pocket pistols of fine workmanship. Shop on Fore Street, Taunton, Somerset.

**Gooch** [about 1750] Shop at Canterbury, Kent. Made flintlock pocket pistols.

**Gooch** [about 1830] General gunsmith at St. Albans, Hertfordshire.

**Goodby, James** [1680–1714] General gunsmith in London.

**Goodwin, George** [1770–1820] Shops at London and Birmingham. Made double barrel, over and under, boxlock flintlock pocket pistols and brass barrel flintlock blunderbuss type pistol with top spring bayonet. Also made flintlock "duck foot" pistol with the four barrels spread like the four fingers of the hand. One lock and hammer and the four barrels fired at one time.

**Gordan** [about 1765] General gunsmith in London.

**Gordon** [about 1590] Established a gunsmithery at Dundee, Scotland.

**Gore** [about 1800] General gunsmith in Liverpool.

**Gorgo** [1660–1680] An Italian craftsman who immigrated to London and established a gunsmithery. Made flintlock three-chambered coach pistols in which the barrels were turned manually. Also made screw barrel flint-lock rifle which was in effect breech-loading.

**Gough, Daniel** [1826–1840] General gunsmith in London. Name changed to **Gough & Bowen** 1840 to 1855.

**Gough, Robert** [about 1715] Shop in London. General gunsmith.

**Gourly** [about 1760] Made flint-lock duelling pistols. Shop in Glasgow.

**Govers** [about 1800] General gunsmith in London.

**Gowling, Frederick** [about 1735] Shop in London. General gunsmith.

**Grainger, T.** [about 1850] Shop in Wolverhampton, Staffordshire. General gunsmith.

**Grant & Sons, Stephen** [1841–1900] Custom gunmakers and dealers at 7 Bury Street, St. James, London. In 1900 merged with **Joseph Lang**.

**Granville, William** [about 1855] General gunsmith in London.

**Graves, William** [1629–1636] One of seven gunsmiths whose name appeared in the text of a commission by Charles I to make Royal arms. Gunsmithery in London.

**Gray** [1750–1800] Made flintlock coach pistols and cased flintlock duelling pistols. Shop in Dublin.

**Gray, Samuel** [about 1850] General gunsmith in London.

**Green** [about 1835] Made cased percussion traveling pistols and double barrel percussion sporting guns. Shop in Canterbury, Kent.

**Green, Abram** [about 1860] Custom gunmaker in London.

**Green, John** [1775–1791] Shop in London. Made flintlock pistols and fowling pieces.

**Green, Thomas** [1680–1720] Made flintlock holster pistols and steel barrel flintlock blunderbusses. Also under Royal Government commission made flintlock military muskets with dog lock. Shop in London.

**Green, William** (5 generations) [1711–1864] General gunsmiths in London. During the period from 1835 to 1864. Made double barrel pill-lock pistols and percussion sporting guns.

**Greener, W.** [1829–1869] Founder of a famous family of gunmakers, W. Greener established a gunsmithery at Newcastle upon Tyne, Northumberland, in 1829, and moved to Aston Manor, Birmingham, in 1844. Opened a London shop at 42 Ely Place, Holborn, London, in 1860. Made mostly long arms, percussion rifles, and sporting guns, later metallic cartridge rifles and shotguns. Name changed to **W. W. Greener** in 1860 to 1879, at 68 Haymarket, London. (W. W. Greener wrote an excellent book on *The Gun and Its Development*.) The name of the firm was again changed to **W. W. Greener & Son** in 1879 located at 40 Pall Mall, London, and St. Mary's Works, Birmingham.

**Greenwood** [about 1800] Shop at Leicester. Made boxlock flintlock pocket pistols with folding trigger.

**Greeves, Joseph** [about 1815] General gunsmith in Birmingham.

**Gregory** [about 1680] Shop in London. Made flintlock muskets with dog lock. Arms carried Royal Cypher.

**Grey & Moore** [1847–1858] Custom gunmakers and dealers in London. Name changed to **William Grey** from 1858 to 1872.

**Grice, William** [1740–1780] Shop in London. Made brass barrel flintlock coach pistols. Also flintlock carbines and muskets with the Royal Cypher.

**Grierson, Charles** [1790–1832] Shop at 10 Bond Street, London. Had the Royal Warrant. Made officers' flintlock holster pistols and flintlock coach pistols of fine workmanship. Most of his pieces had the gold-lined vent in the touchhole to prevent the vent from enlarging due to powder corrosion.

**Griffin, B.** [1739–1773] Shop in Bond Street, London. One of the early makers of double barrel pistols and fowling pieces. Made flintlock pocket and holster pistols with silver mountings, also double barrel, side-by-side, flintlock pistol with two hammers and two triggers. The name became **Griffin & Tow** from 1773 to 1796, continuing on Bond Street. Made cannon barrel flintlock pocket pistols and silver mounted flintlock holster pistols. Also brass barrel flintlock blunderbusses.

**Griffiths, Benjamin** [about 1810] General gunsmith in Birmingham.

**Grimshaw, Thomas** [about 1850] Custom gunmaker in London.

**Grimston, Charles** [about 1820] Shop in London. General gunsmith.

**Grimwade & Co.** [about 1880] Custom gunmakers in London.

**Gritten** [about 1750] General gunsmith in London.

**Groom, Richard** [about 1855] Shop in London. General gunsmith.

**Groves, Jonathan** [about 1795] General gunsmith in Birmingham.

**Grow** [about 1850] Custom gunmaker on the Strand, London.

**Guest, R.** [about 1800] Made flintlock coach pistols with spring bayonet. Shop in Birmingham.

**Gulley, Joseph** [1800–1830] Shop in London. Made flintlock holster pistols.

**Gunby, Osborn & Co.** [1800–1815] Made flintlock holster pistols with swivel ramrod. Shop in London.

**Gurney, Henry** [1854–1864] Custom gunmaker in London.

**Guy, W.** [about 1750] Made cannon barrel, boxlock flintlock pocket pistols. Shop in London.

**Gye & Moncrieff** [1876–1887] Custom gunmakers and importers in London.

# NOTES
## G

**Hacker, Francis** [about **1675**] Established a gunsmithery in London.

**Hackett, Edwin & George** [about **1870**] Custom gunmakers in London.

**Haddon** [**1800–1820**] Shop at Newcastle upon Tyne, Northumberland. General gunsmith.

**Hadley, Gilbert** [about **1740**] General gunsmith at Bristol.

**Hadley, H.** [**1750–1789**] Made brass barrel, bell muzzle, flintlock coach pistols, and double barrel, over and under, flintlock holster pistols, also brass barrel flintlock blunderbusses. Shop in London.

**Hadley, Thomas** [**1750–1770**] General gunsmith in Birmingham.

**Halbeck & Sons** [about **1775**] Made flintlock holster pistols. Shop in London.

**Hale** [about **1770**] General gunsmith in London.

**Hale, Edward & Thomas** [**1810–1819**] Shop in Birmingham. General gunsmith.

**Halfhide, G.** [**1695–1710**] Made cannon barrel, Queen Anne–type, flintlock coach pistols with silver mask butt cap. Shop in London, used "Londini" in marking pieces.

**Hall, Abraham** [about **1650**] Shop in London. Made wheel-lock sporting guns with copper gilt mountings.

**Hall, Collinson** [about **1825**] Made brass barrel flintlock blunderbusses. Shop in London.

**Hall, John** [**1704–1770**] Made cannon barrel, boxlock flintlock pocket pistols and flintlock blunderbusses with Royal Cypher.

**Hall & Powell** [about **1760**] General gunsmith and dealer in Dublin, Ireland.

**Hall, Wasley** [about **1865**] Custom gunmaker in London.

**Halton, Henry** [about **1835**] Shop in Liverpool. General gunsmith.

**Hamburger & Co.** [**1825–1840**] Made flintlock coach pistols and later cased officers' percussion pistols with swivel ramrods and loading equipment. Shop in London.

**Hamilton, John** [about **1630**] Established a gunsmithery in Scotland. Location not known.

**Hammond** [about **1840**] Shop in Winchester, Hampshire. Made percussion traveling pistols with swivel ramrods.

**Hampton, Thomas** [about **1810**] Made flintlock pocket pistols. Shop in Birmingham.

**Hampton, W.** [about **1800**] Shops in London and Birmingham. Made screw barrel flintlock pocket pistols, also brass barrel flintlock blunderbusses with top spring bayonet.

**Hanquet, Ferdinand** [**1870–1882**] Custom gunmaker in London.

**Hanson, Charles** [about **1855**] Made cased percussion pepperboxes with loading equipment. Shop in London.

**Hanson, S.** [about **1830**] General gunsmith in Doncaster, Yorkshire.

**Harcourt, H.** [about **1840**] Shop in Norwich, Norfolk. General gunsmith.

**Harcourt, John** [**1780–1830**] Shop in Ipswich, Suffolk. Made boxlock flintlock pocket pistols and cased flintlock duelling pistols with all accessories. Under Royal Government contract made flintlock holster pistols and blunderbuss type of flintlock naval boarding pistols with spring bayonet.

**Harding, James** [**1750–1815**] Under Royal Government contract made flintlock military holster pistols. Also made flintlock blunderbusses and flintlock full stocked pistols for the coach guards of His Majesty's mail coaches. The pistol and the blunderbuss were numbered the same as a pair, the coach guard carried both arms. The pieces were marked on the lockplate "J. Harding" and on the brass barrel "J. Harding, Borough of London No. _____," at the muzzle end of the barrel "For His Majesty's Mail Coaches." The name became **James Harding & Son** 1815 to 1837.

**Harding, Robert** [1815–1832] Shop in Ludlow, Shropshire. Made cased flintlock traveling pistols with loading equipment.

**Hardwick, T.** [about 1830] General gunsmith at Ross, Hertfordshire.

**Harison, Simon** [about 1715] Shop in London. General gunsmith.

**Harkom, Joseph** [about 1850] Made percussion pepperboxes and cased percussion pistols with sash hooks. Also percussion holster pistols with swivel ramrod. Shop in Edinburgh, Scotland.

**Harley** [about 1850] Shop in London. Made percussion pocket pistols.

**Harman, John** [1720–1750] Made cannon barrel flintlock coach pistols with silver mask butt cap. Also made flintlock fowling pieces with the stock separating into two parts for easy concealment. This was called a "poachers' gun." Shop in London.

**Harold, Victor & Co.** [about 1860] Custom gunmakers in London.

**Harper, I.** [about 1800] Shop in London. General gunsmith.

**Harper, James** [1850–1865] Made percussion pepperboxes and flat bar hammer percussion revolvers. Shop at 85 Weyman Street, London.

**Harris, E.** [about 1800] General gunsmith in Leicester.

**Harris, J.** [about 1750] Shop at Becketts, St. James, London. Made hunting swords with flintlock pistols attached to the hilts.

**Harris, Joseph** [about 1815] General gunsmith in Birmingham.

**Harrison** [about 1800] Made flintlock coach pistols in Manchester.

**Harrison, John** [1725–1774] Shop in London. Made cannon barrel flintlock coach pistols with silver mask butt caps.

**Harrison, John** [about 1765] General gunsmith in Birmingham.

**Harrison, T. & W.** [1840–1860] Shop at Carlisle, Cumberland. Made percussion pepperboxes.

**Harston & Co., G.** [about 1875] Custom gunmakers in London.

**Hart** [1730–1750] Shop in Oxford. Made cannon barrel flintlock coach pistols with silver mask butt caps.

**Hart** [about 1850] General gunsmith in Birmingham.

**Hartwell** [about 1855] Shop at Stow, Gloucestershire. Made double barrel percussion pocket pistols.

**Harvard** [about 1820] General gunsmith in London.

**Harvey** [1840–1853] Shop at Exeter, Devonshire. Developed a hammerless percussion revolver, also made double barrel percussion sporting guns.

**Harvey, Robert** [1690–1725] Made screw barrel, cannon muzzle, flintlock holster pistols. Shop in London.

**Harway** [about 1855] General gunsmith in Birmingham.

**Harwood, John** [about **1835**] Shop at Stokesley, Yorkshire. General gunsmith.

**Hasdell, Thomas R.** [**1852–1866**] Made percussion holster pistols and percussion revolvers. Shop in London.

**Hast, Frederick** [**1856–1870**] Custom gunmaker in London.

**Hast, P.** [**1810–1850**] Shop in Colchester, Essex. Made three-barrel flintlock pocket pistols. Later made percussion traveling pistols and percussion sporting guns.

**Hattersley, Thomas** [about **1830**] General gunsmith at Boston, Lincolnshire.

**Havers, W.** [about **1835**] Shop at Norwich, Norfolk. General gunsmith.

**Hawker** [about **1730**] Made cannon barrel flintlock pocket pistols. Shop in London.

**Hawkes, T.** [about **1830**] General gunsmith in Birmingham.

**Hawkes, William** [about **1835**] Shop at Hull, Yorkshire. General gunsmith.

**Hawkins, John** [**1680–1714**] General gunsmith in London and founder of two generations of gunmakers. His son John, Jr., took over the shop from 1714 to 1760. Made brass barrel, bell muzzle, flintlock holster pistols. General George Washington had a pair by this maker. John Hawkins II carried on the business from 1760 to 1776.

**Haynes, James** [about **1715**] General gunsmith in London.

**Hays** [about **1850**] Made percussion holster pistols. Shop in London.

**Hayward & Goodwin** [about **1780**] Shop in London. Made screw barrel boxlock flintlock pocket pistols with folding trigger.

**Haywood, Peter** [**1775–1820**] Shop in Chester. Made double barrel, over

and under, flintlock pocket pistols. Also made flintlock "duck foot" pistol with the four barrels spread like the four fingers of the hand. One lock and hammer, the four barrels fired at one time.

**Heaps, Thomas A.** [about **1835**] Shop in Huddersfield, Yorkshire. General gunsmith.

**Hearder** [about **1800**] General gunsmith in Plymouth, Devonshire.

**Heasler, Richard & William** [about **1715**] Shop in London. General gunsmiths.

**Heath & Brueton** [about **1765**] General gunsmiths in Birmingham.

**Heath & Hurdd** [about **1770**] Developed a flintlock repeating rifle. Shop in London.

**Heathcote & Evans** [about **1815**] Shop in Birmingham. General gunsmiths.

**Heeley, Richard** [**1767–1790**] Made cased flintlock duelling pistols with loading equipment. Name changed to **John Heeley** (probably Son) 1790 to 1831. Shop in Birmingham.

**Henderson** [about **1860**] Shop in Aberdeen, Scotland. Made boxlock percussion pocket pistols with folding trigger.

**Henneker, E. E.** [**1832–1850**] Made cased percussion pistols with belt hook and of fine workmanship. Also percussion holster pistols with swivel ramrods. Shop at Chatham, Kent.

**Henricke** [about **1590**] Established a gunsmithery in London.

**Henry, Alexander** [**1869–1895**] Shop at 12 Andrews Street, Edinburgh, Scotland. Made percussion sporting, target and match rifles. Later breechloading metallic cartridge rifles. Patented a falling block action breech-loading rifle which competed unsuccessfully with the Martini action in Ordnance Board trials for the British Services. Henry rifles were often given as prizes in Territorial Regimental Shooting Competitions.

**Henshal** [1780–1820] General gunsmith on the Strand, London.

**Henshall, John** [1771–1796] Made flintlock pocket pistols with silver mountings and flintlock holster pistols. Shop in Cambridge.

**Henshall, Thomas** [about 1815] Shop in Birmingham. General gunsmith.

**Henshaw** (2 generations) [1690–1778] Shop in Birmingham. Made flintlock duelling pistols.

**Henshaw, W.** [1780–1820] Under contract for the East India Company, made flintlock holster pistols, brass barrel blunderbuss-type flintlock pistols and heavy wall pivot flintlock guns. Shop on the Strand, London.

**Henson, Thomas** [about 1810] General gunsmith in London.

**Heptinstall, William** [1850–1868] Custom gunmaker in London.

**Herbert, C.** [about 1850] Shop in London. Custom gunmaker.

**Heriot, William** [1758–1773] Made single and double barrel flintlock fowling pieces of fine workmanship. Shop at Edinburgh, Scotland. William Heriot died in 1773.

**Hermann, Edwin** [about 1870] Custom gunmaker in London.

**Hesketh** [about 1800] Made screw barrel flintlock pocket pistols. Shop in London.

**Hetherington, T.** [about 1840] Shop at Nottingham. Made percussion pocket pistols.

**Heutell, Richard** [about 1835] General gunsmith in Liverpool.

**Hewitt, John C.** [1862–1893] Custom gunmaker in London.

**Hewson, Joseph** [about 1790] Made boxlock flintlock pocket pistols. Shop in Exeter, Devonshire.

**Hewson, Thomas** [1830–1860] Shop in Piccadilly, London. Made percussion pocket and holster pistols. Developed a pill-lock double barrel pistol with twelve primer charges in the hammer. Also made cased pairs of percussion traveling pistols with all accessories.

**Heylin, Joseph** [1750–1800] Made brass, cannon barrel, flintlock coach pistols and brass barrel flintlock blunderbusses. Shop in Cornhill, London.

**Heyling, Thomas** [about 1770] General gunsmith in Birmingham.

**Hickes, I.** [1700–1750] Made flintlock pocket pistols. Shop in London.

**Hicking, Joseph** [1767–1779] General gunsmith in Birmingham.

**Hickman** [about 1750] Made boxlock flintlock pocket pistols. Shop in London.

**Higgs** [1775–1808] Shop in London. Made flintlock fowling pieces.

**Higham, G. & E.** [about 1820] Made boxlock flintlock, pocket pistols. Shop in Warrington, Lancashire.

**Higham, S.** [about 1850] Shop at Oswestry, Shropshire. Made cased percussion pistols with belt hook and swivel ramrod.

**Hill** [1750–1780] Made screw barrel, boxlock flintlock pocket pistols and flintlock blunderbuss type of pistol. Shop in London.

**Hill, Abraham** [about 1660] Shop in London. Abraham Hill was granted

Royal Letters of Patent for a gun or pistol that would carry seven or eight charges in sequence in the barrel. Pepys writes in his Diary under date of March 4, 1664, that Lord Sandwich had "a new-fashion gun brought my Lord this morning to shoot often, one after another without trouble or danger."

**Hill & Son, F.** [about 1860] Made a 12-shot metallic cartridge pepperbox type of pistol. Shop at Sheffield, Yorkshire.

**Hill, John** [1820–1856] General gunsmith in London.

**Hill, Thomas** [about 1850] Shop in Inverness, Scotland. Made cased double barrel percussion shotguns with loading and cleaning equipment.

**Hill, W. J.** [1870–1879] Custom gunmaker in London.

**Hind** [about 1800] Shop in Leicester. Made boxlock flintlock pocket pistols.

**Hirst, Jonathan** [1760–1805] Made flintlock breech-loading sporting rifles. These rifles were similar to the Ferguson type, except that the breech plug was removed by turning the trigger guard, which when removed the rifle was turned upside down to load. Also made flintlock heavy wall pivot guns. Shop was located on Tower Hill, London.

**Hobday** [1780–1800] General gunsmith in London. Name changed to **Hobday & Biddle** 1800 to 1826.

**Hobson, Frederick** [about 1815] Made brass barrel flintlock blunderbusses with top spring bayonet. Shop in London.

**Hodges, Perrin & Co.** [about 1860] Custom gunmakers in London.

**Hodges, R. E.** [about 1850] Shop at 44 Southampton Row, London. Custom gunmakers.

**Hodgson** [1790–1835] General gunsmith at Ipswich, Suffolk.

**Hodgson** [about 1805] Made naval flintlock pistols with sash hook and silver mask butt cap. Shop in London.

**Hodgson & Co.** [1840–1850] Custom gunmakers at Newcastle upon Tyne, Northumberland.

**Hoist, L.** [about 1850] Made percussion revolving rifle similar to Colt's. Shop in London.

**Holbrook** [about 1785] General gunsmith in London.

**Holcomb & Lyon** [about 1850] Shop in London. Custom gunmakers and made double barrel percussion shotguns of fine workmanship.

**Holden** [about 1790] General gunsmith in London.

**Holden, John** [about 1835] Shop in Liverpool. General gunsmith.

**Hole, William** [about 1830] General gunsmith in Bristol, Gloucestershire.

**Holland** [about 1860] Custom gunmaker and dealer. Had cased percussion revolvers with his label. Shop in Cirencester, Gloucestershire.

**Holland** [about 1800] General gunsmith in London.

**Holland & Holland** [1835–1900] Shop at 98 New Bond Street, London. Famous pistol and gunmakers. Made percussion revolvers of Adams Patent and metallic cartridge target or match pistols of fine workmanship.

**Holland, H.** [1850–1877] Made double barrel percussion rifles and shotguns. Shop at 9 King Street, Holborn, London. In 1877 merged with

**Holland & Holland** at 98 New Bond Street, London.

**Hollands, Edward [1864–1875]** Custom gunmaker in London.

**Holle** [about **1830**] Shop in London. General gunsmith.

**Holler, A. E. [1858–1870]** Custom gunmaker in London.

**Hollies, Thomas** [about **1720**] General gunsmith in London.

**Hollis & Sons, Isaac [1860–1900]** Made percussion trade muskets under contract for the Hudson's Bay Company. Also under Royal Government contract made percussion rifles and later metallic cartridge carbines with the Snider Patent breech. Shop in London.

**Hollis, Richard W. [1790–1850]** General gunsmith in London. Name became **Richard Hollis & Son** 1850 to 1886. Made all metal percussion Scottish-type pistols with belt hook, and percussion sporting rifles.

**Hollis & Sheath** [about **1850**] Shop in London. Made percussion pocket pistols and percussion double-action revolvers.

**Hollis, William** [about **1770**] Made flintlock pocket pistols and flintlock fowling pieces. Shop on Bath Street, Birmingham.

**Holmes, Henry [1800–1850]** Shop in Liverpool. Made flintlock coach pistols and later percussion pocket pistols with folding trigger and silver mountings.

**Holyoak [1720–1750]** Made flintlock muskets with Royal Cypher. Shop in London.

**Homer, Thomas [1810–1830]** Made screw cannon barrel flintlock coach pistols. These pistols had the barrel, at the breech, fastened to the pistol by a swivel connecting rod, also made flintlock naval pistols with sash hook. Shop in London.

**Hood, Arthur** [about **1830**] General gunsmith at York.

**Hook [1825–1850]** Shop at Tenterden, Kent. Made percussion punt guns and double barrel percussion sporting guns.

**Hopkins, C. W. [1800–1850]** Made flintlock coach pistols with brass mountings and later percussion pistols with belt hook. Shop in London.

**Horsley, Thomas [1834–1880]** Shop at York. Made boxlock percussion pocket pistols and double barrel pinfire shotguns. Also made metallic cartridge .577 caliber breech-loading saddle pistols for big-game hunting.

**Horton, W. [1840–1860]** Made combination percussion rifle and shotgun, the barrels side by side with a 15 gauge shotgun barrel and .60 caliber rifle barrel. Shop at 99 Union Street, Glasgow, Scotland.

**Horton & Waterhouse** [about **1750**] Shop in London. Made double barrel, boxlock flintlock pocket pistols with folding trigger.

**Hosey, John [1668–1700]** General gunsmith in London.

**Hoskins, John** [about **1850**] Custom gunmaker in London.

**Howe [1790–1810]** Made boxlock flintlock pocket pistols and double barrel flintlock fowling pieces, silver mounted and of fine workmanship. Shop at Bristol, Gloucestershire.

**Howell, William** [about **1815**] General gunsmith in Birmingham.

**Hubbard, Michael** [about **1875**] Custom gunmaker in London.

**Hudson, Thomas [1720–1750]** Shop at Temple Bar, London. Made cannon

c

barrel flintlock pocket and coach pistols with silver mask butt caps. Also officers' flintlock holster pistols with silver mountings.

**Huggins, William** [about **1715**] General gunsmith in London.

**Hughes, Daniel** [about **1765**] Shop in Birmingham. General gunsmith.

**Hughes, Robert** [about **1865**] Made percussion sporting guns in London.

**Hughes, T.** [**1710–1730**] General gunsmith in Cork, Ireland.

**Hulbert, C.** [about **1835**] Shop at Shrewsbury, Shropshire. General gunsmithing.

**Hull, T.** [**1810–1820**] General gunsmith in London.

**Humphreys, Charles** [about **1765**] Shop in Birmingham. General gunsmith.

**Hunt, John** [**1760–1779**] Made flintlock pistols with four revolving barrels and one cock and one pan, also Ferguson–type breech-loading flintlock rifles. Shop in London.

**Hunt, Joseph** [about **1765**] General gunsmith in Birmingham.

**Hunt, Thomas** [**1875–1882**] Custom gunmaker in London.

**Hunter** [**1780–1820**] Shop in Edinburgh, Scotland. Made flintlock pistols with belt hook and flintlock holster pistols.

**Hunter, W.** [about **1750**] Made all metal flintlock pistols with scroll butts. Shop in Stirling, Scotland.

**Hurst** [about **1800**] General gunsmith in London.

**Hutchins, John** [about **1865**] Custom gunmaker in London.

**Hutchinson & Lord** [**1775–1820**] Shop in Dublin, Ireland. Made brass frame and brass barrel flintlock pocket pistols.

**Hutchinson, T.** [**1700–1760**] General gunsmithery in London.

**Huzzey, Richard** [about **1880**] Custom gunmaker in London.

**Hyslop** [about **1760**] Shop in London. General gunsmith.

# NOTES
## H

**Ingram, C.** [about **1860**] Shop in Glasgow, Scotland. Made cased double barrel sporting guns.

**Innes** [about **1820**] General gunsmith in Birmingham.

**Innes** [**1770–1790**] Shop at Plymouth, Devon. General gunsmith.

**Innes, Francis** [**1773–1800**] Shop in Edinburgh, Scotland. Had Royal Warrant. Made all metal flintlock pistols with scroll butt and cased flintlock duelling pistols, also made single and double barrel flintlock fowling pieces and Ferguson flintlock breech-loading rifles. Name changed to **Innes & Wallace** 1800 to 1820. Had Royal Government contract for flintlock holster pistols and flintlock muskets.

**Irwin** [about **1850**] Shop in London. Made cased percussion traveling pistols with all accessories.

NOTES

I

Jackson [1780–1830] General gunsmith in London.

Jackson [about 1830] Shop at Maidstone, Kent. General gunsmith.

Jackson, Chris [1714–1750] Made Queen Anne–type flintlock pocket pistols with silver mountings. Shop in London.

Jackson, George [1800–1822] Shop in Birmingham. Made brass three-barrel flintlock pocket pistols.

Jackson, J. [about 1760] Shop at Cranbrook, Kent. Made brass barrel flintlock holster pistols and brass mounted flintlock naval pistols.

Jackson, J. [1800–1830] Made double barrel, over and under, boxlock flintlock pocket pistols with folding trigger, also flintlock holster pistols. Shop at Nottingham.

Jackson, O. [about 1780] Shop at Tenterden, Kent. Made Queen Anne–type flintlock pocket pistols.

Jackson, Richard [1825–1870] Shop in London. Made tube-lock shotguns.

Jackson, Thomas [1850–1879] Made percussion pepperboxes. Shop at 20 Edward Street, Portman Square, London.

Jackson, W. [1835–1850] Shop on Edgware Road, London. Made four-barrel percussion pistols with revolving striker on the hammer, had folding trigger. Also made double barrel percussion rifles.

Jacot, M. & W. [about 1835] General gunsmiths and importers in London.

Jacques [1815–1825] Shop in London. Made flintlock gun firing four superimposed charges using four locks.

Jaeger [about 1750] Made flintlock coach pistols with brass mounts. Shop in London.

James, Enos [1870–1889] Custom gunmaker in London.

James, George [about 1815] Shop in Birmingham. Made flintlock rifles.

James, H. [about 1840] Made percussion holster pistols. Shop in London.

Janssen, J. [1876–1896] Custom gunmaker in London.

Jarrett & Co., Henry T. [about 1870] Dealers and custom gunmakers in London.

Jarvis, W. [1750–1780] General gunsmith in London.

Jeffery & Co., W. J. [1880–1900] Dealer and custom gunmaker at 9 Golden Square, London.

Jefferys [about 1800] Shop at Tadcaster, Yorkshire. Made cased flintlock coach pistols with loading equipment.

Jeffrey, R. [about 1860] Made pinfire double barrel shotguns. Shop on High Street, Guildford, Surrey.

Jeffries [about 1865] General gunsmithing at Norwich, Norfolk.

Jobson, George [about 1835] Shop at Newcastle upon Tyne, Northumberland. General gunsmith.

Johnson [about 1750] Made flintlock pocket pistols and brass barrel flintlock blunderbusses with spring bayonet. Shop at Newcastle upon Tyne, Northumberland.

Johnson & Collins [about 1810] Made flintlock pocket pistols and steel barrel flintlock blunderbusses. Shop at Birmingham.

Johnson, G. [about 1800] Made flintlock breech-loading rifles similar to the Ferguson pattern. Located in London.

Johnson, John [about 1715] Shop in London. General gunsmithing.

**Johnston, Richard** [1810–1820] Made screw barrel flintlock pocket pistols and flintlock coach pistols. Shop on St. James Street, London.

**Johnstone, Patrick** [1820–1835] General gunsmith in London.

**Jonas** [about 1680] Made flintlock muskets with Royal Cypher. Shop in London.

**Jonas, John** [1806–1815] General gunsmith in Birmingham.

**Jones, Charles** [1835–1860] Shop at 32 Cockspur Street, London. Made percussion pepperboxes and four-barrel percussion pistols with two hammers and two nipples, the barrels revolved. Also patented a percussion lock in which the percussion cap fitted in the head of the hammer instead of on the nipple. Also made percussion sporting guns.

**Jones, G.** [1689–1720] Shop in London. General gunsmithing.

**Jones, George** [1813–1827] General gunsmith in Birmingham.

**Jones, George E.** [1790–1810] General gunsmith in London.

**Jones, I.** [1700–1725] Made brass barrel flintlock blunderbusses and flintlock musketoons, both with Royal Cypher. Shop in London.

**Jones, J. N.** [about 1740] Shop in London. Made screw barrel boxlock flintlock pocket pistols and flintlock fowling pieces; also flintlock holster pistols, these with Royal Cypher.

**Jones, John** [1780–1823] Made double barrel, over and under, rifled flintlock pocket pistols, also naval officers' combination cutlass and flintlock pistols, the boxlock pistol in the hilt and the barrel on the top of the blade. Made flintlock rifles with Royal Cypher. Shop in Cornhill, London.

**Jones, John** [about 1840] Shop in Liverpool. Made double barrel percussion sporting guns.

**Jones, Robert** [1844–1860] Made all metal Scottish-type percussion dress pistols and double-action percussion revolvers. Shop at 3 Great Howard Street, Liverpool.

**Jones, Thomas** [1750–1770] Shop in London. Made brass barrel flintlock blunderbusses.

**Jones, Thomas** [1832–1850] Shop at Wrexham, Wales. Made cased small caliber boxlock, percussion, folding trigger pistols. These were known as ladies' "muff" pistols.

**Jones, William** [1812–1842] Shop in London. Made flintlock holster pistols with swivel ramrod and later large bore percussion hunting pistols.

**Jordan** [1733–1760] Made flintlock holster pistols and flintlock Grenadiers' muskets, both with Royal Cypher. Shop in London.

**Joseph, I.** [about 1790] Shop in Liverpool. Made double barrel, over and under, boxlock flintlock pocket pistols.

**Joseph & Co., Solomon** [1870–1886] Custom gunmakers and dealers in London.

**Josephs, William** [about 1810] General gunsmith in Birmingham.

**Jover, William** [1750–1786] Shop in London. Made three-barrel flintlock pocket pistols with one cock and one pan. Also made cased flintlock duelling and coach pistols. Made flintlock dragoon pistols with Royal Cypher, and brass barrel flintlock blunderbusses. Name changed to **Jover & Belton** 1786 to 1810.

**Joyner** [1765–1810] Made brass barrel, bell muzzle, flintlock coach pistols and brass barrel flintlock blunderbusses. Also flintlock carbines with Royal Cypher. Shop in London.

# NOTES
## J

**Kavanagh, W. & J.** [1830–1862] Shop at 12 Dane Street, Dublin, Ireland. Made double barrel, over and under, percussion pistols with swivel ramrod and pin-fire shotguns. Later they handled percussion revolvers.

**Keen, Job** [about 1850] General gunsmith in London.

**Keene, John William** [about 1815] Shop in Birmingham. General gunsmith.

**Kellie, Alexander** [about 1835] General gunsmithing at Hexham, Northumberland.

**Kemp Bros.** [1850–1860] Custom gunmakers in London. Name changed to **Kemp, Leddall & Co.** 1860 to 1872.

**Kendall** [about 1860] Shop at Windsor, Berkshire. Made underhammer percussion coach pistols.

**Kendall, Joseph** [about 1765] General gunsmith at Birmingham.

**Kennedy** [1775–1827] Shop at Kilmarnock, Scotland. General gunsmithing.

**Kent & Co.** [about 1820] Made flintlock coach pistols. Shop in London.

**Kerr & Co.** [1855–1894] Owned by two brothers, John and James Kerr. They had shops in London and Birmingham. John Kerr patented in December 1858, a single-action percussion revolver. This was a solid frame arm with the cylinder pin withdrawn from the rear and the rammer under the barrel. Two models were made .44 caliber and .38 caliber both with 5½-inch barrels. In 1859 a double-action revolver was patented. These were not as popular in England as the Adams or Tranter percussion revolvers but had a good market abroad. Officially adopted by the Portuguese Army and also imported by the Con-federate States of America during the Civil War.

**Kerrison, John** [1830–1855] Made double barrel percussion coach pistols. Shop at Wrexham, Wales.

**Ketland, William & William** (Grandson) [1740–1804] William Ketland, Sr., established a gunsmithy at Birmingham in 1740, and after his death, of which no record has been found to date, his eldest grandson, William Ketland, carried on the business until his death in 1804. During this period they operated under the name of **Ketland & Co.** It is not definitely known when they opened the London shop but believed about 1760, and were one of the first Birmingham gunmakers to compete with the London makers of fine workmanship. The Ketland arms mark later developed into the Birmingham Proof Mark. William Ketland II's brother-in-law, Thomas Izon continued to operate the company under the name **Ketland & Co.** until 1831, when they got into financial difficulties and the firm ceased operations.

William Ketland, Sr., had two other grandsons, Thomas and John Ketland, both gunsmiths who worked on a co-operative basis with William Ketland under the name of **Ketland & Co.** However, Thomas and John emigrated to the United States in 1789 and settled in Philadelphia, Pennsylvania. A number of American Kentucky rifles had **Ketland & Co.** locks.

**Ketland & Co.** flintlock pistols and fowling pieces, are noted for their fine workmanship and design, and the company also manufactured parts and tools for other gunsmiths.

The names **Ketland & Ryding** (1790) and **Ketland, Walker & Adams** (1750–1815) appear on some pieces and were probably again co-operative arrangements.

**Kew** [about 1840] Shop at Louth, Lincolnshire. Made boxlock percussion pocket pistols.

**Key, A.** [about 1800] Made double barrel flintlock holster pistols. Shop at St. Andrews, Scotland.

**Kimbley** [about 1750] General gunsmith in London.

**Kimbley, B.** [about 1830] Shop at Leeds, Yorkshire. General gunsmith.

**King, J.** [1770–1790] Made screw cannon barrel flintlock pocket pistols and brass barrel flintlock blunderbusses. Also flintlock muskets with Royal Cypher. Shop in London.

**King, Richard** [1690–1702] Shop in London (used "Londini" in marking his pieces). Made cannon barrel flintlock coach pistols with silver mask butt cap.

**King, T. J.** [about 1850] Made boxlock percussion pocket pistols of fine workmanship. Shop at Bristol, Gloucestershire.

**Kipling, Charles & Richard** [about 1715] Established a gunsmithery in London.

**Kirk, W.** [1764–1790] Shops in London and Birmingham. General gunsmith.

**Kirke, J.** [1770–1780] Made flintlock fowling pieces. Shop at Warsop, Nottinghamshire.

**Kirkham, Henry** [about 1715] General gunsmithing in London.

**Kitching** [about 1820] General gunsmith at Darlington, Durham.

**Kleft, W. H.** [1780–1820] Shop in London. General gunsmith.

**Knight** [about 1815] General gunsmithing. Shop at Bristol, Gloucestershire.

**Knight, Y.** [about 1800] Shop at Oxford. General gunsmith.

**Knubley** [1750–1799] Made boxlock flintlock pocket pistols with detachable dagger, and cased flintlock duelling pistols with loading accessories. Also made the Ferguson-type flintlock breech-loading pistols. Under Royal Government contract made flintlock carbines. Shop in London.

**Kolbe** [1750–1800] General gunsmith in London.

**Koster** [about 1620] Established a gunsmithery in London.

**Krauss, Paul** [1871–1883] Custom gunmaker in London.

**Kynoch Gun Factory** [about 1860] Plant at Aston, Warwickshire. Made percussion sporting guns.

**Kysling, Richard** [about 1710] Established a gunsmithery in London.

# NOTES

## K

**Lacy & Co.** [1776–1840] (Bennett Lacy and J. G. Lacy) Shop in London. Made flintlock holster pistols and flintlock muskets under Royal Government contract. Later made double barrel, over and under, percussion pistols with swivel ramrods and belt hook. Name changed to **Lacy & Reynolds** from 1840 to 1853. Made percussion pepperboxes.

**Ladmore, E.** [1825–1840] Shop at Hereford. Made double barrel, rifled, "turn over" percussion pistols and percussion pepperboxes.

**Laing** [about 1860] Shop at Edinburgh, Scotland. Made cased double barrel percussion sporting guns.

**Laird, J. W.** [about 1870] Made percussion pocket pistols with detachable daggers. Shop in London.

**Lakin** [about 1850] Made percussion pocket pistols. Shop at Tamworth, Staffordshire.

**Lambe, J.** [1700–1725] Made breech-loading flintlock rifles which had a screw plug at the top of the breech that was withdrawn by a tool attached with a chain. Shop at Salisbury, Wiltshire.

**Lambert** [about 1780] Shop in London. Made four-barrel, rifled, boxlock flintlock pocket pistols with one cock. These are of fine workmanship.

**Lamblin & Co., L.** [1868–1893] Custom gunmakers in London.

**Lancaster, Charles William** (2 generations) [1826–1867] Shop at 151 New Bond Street, London. Made double barrel flintlock fowling pieces. Later made saw-handle percussion duelling pistols, cased percussion traveling pistols with loading accessories, and percussion pepperboxes. Under Royal Government contract made percussion military rifles. For civilian trade made four-barrel "turn over" rifles and cased double barrel percussion sporting guns with all accessories. Name changed to **Charles Lancaster & Co.** from 1867 to 1900. Made four-barrel .476 caliber metallic cartridge pistols for big-game hunting. In 1900 the company merged with Stephen Grant & Sons and Joseph Lang & Co., Ltd.

**Landell, W.** [about 1840] Made percussion sporting rifles. Shop at Glasgow, Scotland.

**Lane** [about 1780] Shop at Brighton, Sussex. General gunsmith.

**Lane & Freeman** [about 1815] General gunsmiths in London.

**Lane, George J.** [about 1875] Custom gunmaker in London.

**Lane, T.** [about 1830] Shop in Worcester. General gunsmith.

**Lane, Thomas** [1760–1770] General gunsmith in Birmingham.

**Lane, Thomas** [1700–1730] Made cannon barrel flintlock pocket pistols. Shop in London.

**Lang, Edward** [about 1880] Custom gunmaker in London.

**Lang, James** [about 1885] Shop at 22 Cockspur Street, London. Custom gunmaker and metallic cartridge target rifles of fine workmanship.

**Lang, Joseph** [1821–1874] Shop at 7 Haymarket, London. General gunsmith and dealer in percussion short and long arms and later metallic cartridge arms. Name changed to **Joseph Lang & Son** 1874 to 1896, and to **Lang & Hussey** 1896 to 1900 when Charles Lancaster & Co. and Stephen Grant & Sons merged with them under the name of **Joseph Lang & Co., Ltd.**

**Laugher, C. & J.** [1800–1820] Made screw barrel flintlock pocket pistols with under spring bayonet, and brass barrel flintlock blunderbusses with top spring bayonet. Shop in Birmingham.

**Lawdell** [1800–1830] Shop in Lewes, Sussex. General gunsmithing.

**Lawrie, J.** [about 1835] General gunsmith at Leicester.

**Lawson, J.** [about 1860] Shop in Glasgow, Scotland. Custom gunmaker and dealer of Tranter Patent percussion revolvers.

**Lawton, A.** [1861–1876] Custom gunmaker in London.

**Laycock, Samuel** [about 1835] Shop at Sheffield, Yorkshire. General gunsmith.

**Lee, Thomas** [about 1850] Under Royal Government contract made percussion muskets. Shop in London.

**Lees, James** [about 1850] Shop in Perth, Scotland. Made cased double barrel percussion sporting guns.

**Leigh, James** [1812–1832] General gunsmith in London.

**Leigh, John** [1850–1864] Custom gunmaker in London.

**Leitch, James** [about 1860] Shop in London. General gunsmith.

**Lemman** [about 1815] General gunsmithing. Shop at Battle, Sussex.

**Leonard, D.** [about 1880] Shop in Birmingham. Custom gunmaker.

**Levy & Co.** [1830–1840] Gunsmiths and dealers in Bristol, Gloucestershire.

**Lewis, T.** [about 1835] General gunsmithing. Shop at Carmarthen, Wales.

**Lewis & Tomes** [1840–1860] Made percussion pocket pistols. Shop in London.

**Liddell** [about 1780] Shop at Durham. Made three-barrel flintlock pocket pistols with center hammer and one pan.

**Lill** [about 1840] Made percussion pocket pistols. Shop at Louth, Lincolnshire.

**Lindsay, A.** [about 1825] Shop in London. General gunsmithing.

**Ling, William** [1850–1865] Made cased percussion pepperboxes with all loading and cleaning accessories. Shop in Jermyn Street, London.

**Little, Robert** [1800–1815] General gunsmith in Birmingham.

**Littley, Thomas** [about 1835] Shop in Sheffield, Yorkshire. General gunsmith.

**Liversidge, J.** [about 1840] General gunsmith in Birmingham.

**Lloyd, Thomas** [about 1850] Shops in London and Lewes, Sussex. Made percussion traveling pistols and cased pairs of percussion duelling pistols. Also percussion sporting guns.

**Lobcery** [about 1700] Established a gunsmithery at Winchester, Southampton.

**Lock, Arthur** [1800–1815] General gunsmith in London.

**Lockhart, John** [about 1605] Established a gunsmithery in Scotland. Location not known.

**Loder, Edward & Richard** [1750–1793] Under contract for the East India Company made heavy flintlock ships' swivel guns. Shop in London.

**Logane, Alexander** [1658–1670] General gunsmith in Scotland. Location not known.

**Lombard & Butler** [about 1825] Shop in London. Custom gunmakers.

**London Armoury Co.** [1856–1880] Formed by John and Robert Adams and John Kerr with the help of outside capital. Under Royal Government contracts made the Beaumont–Adams percussion revolvers and the Kerr Patent (December 1858) percussion revolvers. Later made the same models in metallic cartridge revolvers. Plant located at 24 Holborn, London.

**London, Edward** [1840–1872] Shop at 51 London Wall, London. Made percussion duelling pistols with silver mountings, also percussion sporting guns.

**London, William** [1825–1840] Made screw cannon barrel flintlock pocket pistols. Shop in London.

**Loneux, Andrew** [about 1865] Custom gunmaker and importer in London.

**Long & Co., Richard** [about 1870] Shop in London. Custom gunmaker.

**Long, Thomas** [about 1770] General gunsmith in Birmingham.

**Longley** [about 1840] Made percussion traveling pistols. Shop in London.

**Lord, T.** [about 1775] Shop in Dublin, Ireland. Made flintlock duelling pistols with silver mounts.

**Lord, William** [about 1715] Shop in London. General gunsmithing.

**Lordon** [about 1745] General gunsmith at London.

**Lott** [about 1780] Shop at Canterbury, Kent. Made screw barrel flintlock coach pistols.

**Lott** [1800–1820] Made double barrel flintlock coach pistols with two hammers and two triggers. Also naval boarding flintlock pistols with bell muzzle and spring bayonet. Shop in Reading, Berkshire.

**Lough, Thomas** [about 1835] General gunsmith at Berwick, Scotland.

**Lovat, Thomas** [about 1830] Shop at Ripon, Yorkshire. General gunsmith.

**Love, Samuel** [1677–1689] Shop in London. General gunsmithing.

**Low, James** [about 1730] Made flintlock holster pistols with silver mountings and mask butt caps of fine workmanship. Shop in London.

**Lowdell** [1800–1820] Shop at Lewes, Sussex. General gunsmith.

**Lowe, C.** [1760–1800] Made brass barrel, blunderbuss-type naval flintlock pistols. Shop in London.

**Lowe, Samuel** [1730–1780] Shop in London. Made flintlock traveling pistols with silver lion mask butt caps.

**Lowe, Thomas** [1767–1780] Made brass barrel flintlock blunderbusses with top spring bayonet. Shop in Birmingham.

**Lowe, Thomas** [about 1840] Shop in Chester. Made percussion pocket pistols.

**Loyd, Evan** [about 1715] Established a gunsmithery in London.

**Lukey** [about 1785] General gunsmith in Birmingham.

**Luneschloss, John D.** [about 1860] Custom gunmaker in London.

**Lyell, J.** [about 1850] Shop at Aberdeen, Scotland. Made silver plated Scottish-type percussion dress pistols with scroll butt and belt hook. Also made cased double barrel percussion shotguns with all accessories.

## NOTES
### L

**Mabson & Labron** [1832–1850] Formerly **Dunderdale, Mabson & Labron.** Made percussion short and long arms at Birmingham.

**Mace, L.** [1800–1820] Shop at Reading, Berkshire. Made flintlock pocket and traveling pistols. Name changed to **Mace & Evans** from 1820 to 1835.

**MacDonell** [about 1750] Made all metal flintlock pistols with scroll butt. Shop at Glengarry, Scotland.

**Mac Guire, John** [1865–1887] Custom gunmakers in London.

**Machie, James** [1879–1893] Shop in London. Custom gunmakers.

**MacLauchlan** [about 1790] Made double barrel, over and under, flintlock pocket pistols. Shop in Edinburgh, Scotland.

**MacLeod** [1711–1750] Made all metal flintlock pistols with scroll butt. Shop at Doune, Scotland.

**Malbon, C.** [about 1815] Shop at Chester. General gunsmith.

**Manchester Ordnance Rifle Co.** [about 1865] Had Royal Government contracts and foreign government contracts for military rifles. Plant at Manchester, Lancashire.

**Mann, William** [1775–1790] Shop in Gorbals, Glasgow, Scotland. Made flintlock pocket pistols with walnut stocks.

**Manners, Edward** [about 1845] General gunsmith in London.

**Manning** [about 1750] Shop in Salop, location not known. General gunsmith.

**Manning, James** [about 1830] General gunsmith. Shop at North Walsham, Norfolk.

**Manton, John** [1780–1820] The elder of two brothers who were famous gunsmiths in London. John Manton marked his pieces "Manton" on the lock plate and "Manton London" on the barrel whilst his younger brother Joseph inscribed his with the full name. John Manton established his shop at 6 Dover Street, London. Made double barrel flintlock fowling pieces, and large caliber hunting rifles. Also made heavy pivot flintlock wall guns. The name was changed to **John Manton & Son** at the same address 1820 to 1834. Made percussion holster pistols.

**Manton, Joseph** [1795–1835] Joseph Manton born 1766 was the younger brother of John Manton, famous London gunmaker. John Manton marked his pieces "Manton London," while Joseph Manton used the full name for identification. Joseph Manton established a gunshop at 27 Davies Street, Berkeley Square, London, in 1795. He was noted for his fine craftsmanship in cased duelling pistols, fowling pieces, heavy-game guns, and rifles, both flintlock and percussion. One of his contributions to the flintlock arm was the V-shaped priming pan which he introduced about 1800 and about this time patented the "elevating rib" on double barrel pieces, both fowling pieces and pistols. In 1816 he patented the percussion "pellett lock" which Forsyth claimed was an infringement, and Forsyth won the court decision. In 1818 Joseph Manton patented the percussion "tube lock" which was not successful and did not gain popularity.

Colonel Peter Hawker of Longparish, Hampshire, sportsman and author of *Instructions to Young Sportsmen,* said that he "was a patron of Joseph Manton and made many field trials of his guns, and contributed to the design and inventions of Joseph Manton." Colonel Hawker, who was a Lieutenant Colonel of the North

Hampshire Regiment and wounded in the Peninsular Campaign, also claims to have induced Joseph Manton to make a copper percussion cap, another claimant to this final development of the percussion system. Joseph Manton was active in the business until he died on June 29, 1835, and is buried at Kensal Green outside of London. His son carried on the business after his death, and the firm name was **Joseph Manton & Son Company.** About 1840 they moved to 116 Jermyn Street. Also about this time they opened a Calcutta, India, branch. The firm ceased operations in 1877.

**Mapplebeck & Lowe** [1840–1855] General gunsmiths in London.

**Mares** [about 1855] A former Armourer Sergeant of the 16th Lancers established his own gunshop in London. Made officers' percussion holster pistols.

**Marnes, T.** [1850–1868] Custom gunmaker in London.

**Marnes, William** [about 1870] Shop in London. General gunsmith.

**Marrison** [1830–1850] Made five-cylinder percussion pepperboxes. These were rotated by hand. Shop at Norwich, Norfolk.

**Marshall** [1750–1798] Shop in London. Made brass barrel flintlock blunderbusses.

**Marshall & Sons** [about 1750] Made all metal flintlock pistols with scroll butts and ball trigger. Shop in Edinburgh, Scotland.

**Marson & Co., Samuel** [1840–1900] Under Royal Government contract made percussion carbines. Shop on Livery Street, Birmingham.

**Marson, T.** [1760–1810] Made brass barrel flintlock blunderbusses. Shop in London.

**Martin** [about 1840] Shop in Paisley, Scotland. Made boxlock percussion pistols.

**Martin, Alexander** [about 1850] General gunsmith at Glasgow, Scotland.

**Martin, G. H.** [about 1800] Made flintlock pocket pistols with silver mountings. Shop in London.

**Martyn** [about 1790] Established a gunsmithery in London.

**Marwood, William** [about 1810] General gunsmith in London.

**M'Ary** [about 1830] Shop at Newbury, Berkshire. General gunsmith.

**Mason, W. & D.** [1750–1790] Made flintlock duelling pistols. Shop in London.

**Masu, Gustave** [1864–1882] Custom gunmaker and importer in London.

**Mather** [1800–1825] Made flintlock duelling pistols. Shop at Newcastle upon Tyne, Northumberland.

**Matherbe, Joseph Philip** [1854–1858] Custom gunmaker in London. Name became **Matherbe, Prosper & Co.** 1858 to 1869.

**Matthews, William** [about 1830] Shop at Penrith, Cumberland. General gunsmith.

**Maullin** [1750–1810] Made rifled screw barrel flintlock pocket pistols and brass barrel flintlock coach pistols. Shop in London.

**Maybury & Co.** [about 1840] Shop in Birmingham. Made percussion pepperboxes and percussion holster pistols.

**Mayer** [about 1850] General gunsmith at Norwich, Norfolk.

**Mayo, Samuel** [about 1810] Shop in Birmingham. General gunsmithing.

**Mazor, J.** [about **1830**] General gunsmith at Yarmouth, Norfolk.

**McAlaster, John** [about **1650**] Established a gunsmithery in Scotland. Location not known.

**McAllan** [**1750–1763**] Made all metal flintlock pistols with scroll butt. Shop in Edinburgh, Scotland.

**McCormick** [**1800–1815**] Shop in Belfast, Ireland. General gunsmithing.

**McCulloch, Charles** [**1725–1740**] Made brass barrel, steel stock, flintlock pistols with scroll butt. Shop at Inverness, Scotland.

**McDermott** [**1790–1840**] Shop in Dublin, Ireland. Made flintlock coach pistols with silver mountings and double barrel flintlock fowling pieces of fine workmanship. Later percussion holster pistols with swivel ramrod.

**McEwen** [about **1800**] General gunsmith at Edinburgh, Scotland.

**McGill, J.** [about **1810**] Made brass barrel flintlock blunderbusses. Shop at Dublin, Ireland.

**McKenzie, D.** [**1700–1725**] Shop in London. General gunsmithing.

**McKenzie, David & James** (son) [**1707–1750**] Shop at Dundee, Scotland. Made all metal flintlock pistols, some with heart-shaped butts and later scroll butts. David McKenzie died in 1728 and his son, James carried on the gunsmithery.

**McKenzie, James** [about **1750**] Shop at Brechin, Scotland. Made all metal flintlock pistols with scroll butts. Also flintlock fowling pieces and muskets.

**McKlellane, John** [about **1615**] Established a gunsmithery in Scotland. Location not known.

**McKnight** [**1835–1855**] Made cased saw-handle percussion duelling pistols

with loading equipment. Shop in Dublin, Ireland.

**McNab, Patrick** [**1725–1750**] Shop at Dalmally, Scotland. Made all metal flintlock pistols with scroll butts.

**McRosty, James** [**1700–1725**] Made all metal flintlock pistols with scroll butts. Shop at Edinburgh, Scotland.

**McWilliam, J. T.** [about **1860**] Custom gunmaker in London.

**Meevis, William** [about **1765**] Shop in Birmingham. General gunsmith.

**Melland, G.** [**1861–1876**] Shop in London. Custom gunmaker.

**Memory** [**1792–1810**] Made Queen Anne–type flintlock coach pistols with brass mask butt caps, and flintlock heavy wall pivot guns. Shop in London.

**Meredith** [**1810–1840**] Made double barrel flintlock fowling pieces, and, later, percussion traveling pistols. Shop in London.

**Meredith** [about **1790**] Shop in Chester. Made screw barrel flintlock pocket pistols and officers' flintlock holster pistols.

**Mewburn & Co.** [about **1875**] Custom gunmakers in London.

**Mewis & Moseley** [about **1790**] Made flintlock pocket pistols with silver mountings and brass barrel flintlock blunderbusses. Shop in Birmingham.

**Meyer & Quiller** [**1770–1800**] Shop at Edinburgh, Scotland. Made all metal flintlock pistols with scroll butts and belt hooks.

**Michie, George and James** [**1725–1750**] Made all metal flintlock pistols with scroll butts. Shop at Doune, Scotland.

**Miles** [**1830–1855**] Shop in London. Made cased flintlock and later percussion traveling pistols with loading accessories. Fine workmanship.

**Millar, John & James** (son) [1688–1731] General gunsmiths at Edinburgh, Scotland.

**Millard, William** [about 1770] Shop in Birmingham. General gunsmithing.

**Mills, W.** [1810–1860] Made Scottish-type all metal flintlock pistols with scroll butts and flintlock pocket pistols. Later made cased percussion traveling and duelling pistols, also percussion holster pistols with swivel ramrod. Made percussion sporting guns of fine workmanship. Shop at 120 High Holborn, London.

**Milton** [about 1850] Shop in London. Made cased percussion traveling pistols with loading equipment.

**Mitchel, John** [1725–1750] Made brass barrel, steel stock flintlock pistols with heart-shaped butts. Shop at Edinburgh, Scotland.

**Mitchell, William** [about 1660] Established a gunsmithery in Scotland. Location not known.

**Moggridge, J. J.** [about 1850] Custom gunmaker in London.

**Moll, P. & D.** [about 1800] Made officers' flintlock holster pistols. Shop in London.

**Monck, J.** [about 1830] General gunsmith at Stamford, Lincolnshire.

**Monlong** [about 1700] Shop in London. A French émigré from Paris who came over after the revocation of the Edict of Nantes in 1685. Noted for the exceptional decoration and design of his arms. An example is a pair of flintlock pistols with walnut stocks, overall length 18 inches, barrels 11 inches, bore $^9/_{16}$ inches. Steel mountings etched with foliage and butt caps damascened in gold.

**Moody** [about 1780] Made flintlock holster pistols in London.

**Moor, John** [about 1765] Shop in Birmingham. General gunsmithing.

**Moore** [about 1840] Made boxlock percussion pocket pistols. Shop at Chichester, Sussex.

**Moore, Charles** [1780–1835] Shop at 77 St. James Street, London. Made officers' flintlock holster pistols with side spring bayonet and flintlock fowling pieces of fine workmanship. Later, made cased percussion duelling pistols with detonator in nose of hammer.

**Moore, Daniel** [1750–1801] Made screw cannon barrel flintlock pocket pistols with masked butt caps. Under contract with the East India Company made flintlock holster pistols and flintlock muskets. Shop in London.

**Moore, G.** [about 1840] Shop in London. Made cased double barrel percussion sporting guns with loading and cleaning equipment.

**Moore & Grey** [1853–1890] (William Moore & William Grey) Shop at 43 Bond Street, London. Custom gunmakers and made metallic cartridge target pistols.

**Moore, S.** [1689–1730] Shop in London. General gunsmithing.

**Moore, Thomas** [about 1690] Established a gunsmithery in London.

**Moore, William** [1790–1835] Shop at 78 Edgware Road, London. An early maker of rifled flintlock pistols, made cased traveling pistols, also flintlock swivel boat guns. Later percussion duelling pistols and percussion sporting guns. Under Royal Government contract made percussion muskets.

**Moore, Williams & Co.** [1854–1872] Custom gunmakers in London. Made a combination percussion rifle and shotgun, barrels side by side, .36 caliber rifle barrel and 12 gauge shotgun barrel.

**Moore & Woodward** [1850–1870] Shop in London. Custom gunmakers.

**Morfat, John** [about 1850] Made percussion pocket pistols. Shop on Scotland Street, Birmingham.

**Morgan, William** [about 1865] Shop in London. Made percussion pocket pistols.

**Morris, Henry** [about 1810] General gunsmith in Birmingham.

**Morris, Isaac** [about 1715] Shop in London. General gunsmithing.

**Morris, William** [about 1780] General gunsmith at Perth, Scotland.

**Morter, William** [about 1830] Shop at North Walsham, Norfolk. General gunsmith.

**Mortimer, D.** [1830–1845] General gunsmith in London.

**Mortimer, H. W.** [1780–1835] Shop at 89 Fleet Street, London. Had Royal Warrant. Under Royal Government contract was one of the early makers of flintlock pistols and blunderbusses for the guards of the Royal mail coaches. Made officers' flintlock holster pistols and cased sets of flintlock duelling pistols with loading accessories. Also flintlock fowling pieces and rifles. Name changed to **H. W. Mortimer & Son** 1835 to 1855.

**Mortimer, Jackson** [1790–1820] Under Royal Government contract, made flintlock muskets. Shop in London.

**Mortimer, Thomas Elsworth** [1851–1867] Shops at 34 St. James Street, London and 97 George Street, Edinburgh, Scotland. Made cased double barrel percussion traveling pistols

with loading accessories; and percussion revolvers, Adams Patent.

**Mortimer & Son, Thomas J.** [1820–1852] Shop at 44 Ludgate Hill, London. Made double barrel flintlock holster pistols. Later, officers' percussion holster pistols and cased percussion duelling pistols with loading equipment. Also double barrel percussion shotguns of fine workmanship.

**Morton** [about 1780] Shop in Dublin, Ireland. Made brass barrel flintlock blunderbusses.

**Morton, B.** [1770–1800] General gunsmith in Birmingham.

**Morton, William** [about 1875] Custom gunmaker in London.

**Moseley, John** [about 1810] Shop in Birmingham. General gunsmith.

**Mosley, Edward** [about 1830] General gunsmith at Sheffield, Yorkshire.

**Mould, James** [about 1825] Shop in London. General gunsmithing.

**Moxham, Thomas** [1802–1820] Made cased saw-handle flintlock duelling pistols with loading equipment. Shop in Birmingham.

**Mozeen, Samuel** [about 1835] General gunsmith at Hull, Yorkshire.

**Mozley** [about 1750] Made screw brass barrel boxlock flintlock pocket pistols. Shop in London.

**Muler, Martin** [1689–1710] Shop in London. General gunsmithing.

**Muley** [1760–1795] Made four-barrel flintlock pocket pistols and brass barrel, bell muzzle, flintlock coach pistols. Also brass barrel flintlock blunderbusses. Shop in Dublin, Ireland.

**Mundy & Co., P. F.** [about 1820] General gunsmiths in Birmingham.

**Murcott, Theophilus** [1861–1878] Custom gunmaker in London.

**Murdoch, Alexander** [1750–1775] Made all metal flintlock pistols with lobe-shaped butts. Shop in Edinburgh, Scotland.

**Murdoch, James** (father and son) [1714–1760] Shop in Inverness, Scotland. Made all metal flintlock pistols. Those made by Murdoch the elder had a very light belt hook and the whole barrel had a chased design. Those made by the son, only the muzzle of the barrel was chase designed and they also carried a strong wide belt hook.

**Murdoch, John** [1750–1798] Shop at Doune, Scotland. Made all metal flint-lock pistols with scroll butts and acorn triggers. Some were made with gilt brass stock and butt. The flintlock pistols of Major John Pitcairn, Royal Marines, at Lexington and Concord, April 19, 1775, were by this maker.

**Murdoch, Thomas** [1730–1785] Made all metal (some all brass) flintlock pistols with lobe-shaped butts. Shop at Leith, Scotland.

**Murphy** [about 1790] Shop in Dublin, Ireland. Made officers' flintlock holster pistols.

**Mustow, R. J.** [about 1855] General gunsmith in London.

# NOTES
## M

**Nairn** [about **1750**] Shop in Edinburgh, Scotland. General gunsmithing.

**Naylor** [about **1845**] Made percussion traveling pistols. Shop at Sheffield, Yorkshire.

**Naylor, Isaac** [**1833–1851**] Shop at Barnsley, Yorkshire. General gunsmith.

**Needham, Joseph & Henry** [**1856–1880**] Made double barrel percussion shotguns and later double barrel needle-fire shotguns. Shop in London.

**Needham & Co., T.** [**1870–1890**] Shop in London. Made cartridge shotguns with early type of patented (1874) cartridge ejector.

**Needham, William** [**1843–1853**] General gunsmith in London.

**Neill, J.** [about **1850**] Shop at Belfast, Ireland. Made double barrel, over and under, percussion pocket pistols.

**Nelson, J.** [**1710–1730**] Shop at Portsmouth, Hampshire. General gunsmithing.

**Nevill** [about **1810**] Made cannon barrel flintlock pocket pistols and cased duelling pistols with loading accessories. Shop in London.

**New, H.** [**1812–1835**] General gunsmith in Birmingham.

**New, H.** [**1750–1780**] Made double barrel, over and under, boxlock flintlock pistols and flintlock coach pistols of fine workmanship. Shop in London.

**Newby, Edwin Henry** [**1867–1890**] Custom gunmaker in London.

**Newton** [**1770–1815**] Famous gunsmith at Grantham, Lincolnshire. Noted for fine workmanship. Made cannon barrel boxlock flintlock pocket pistols, Queen Anne–type flintlock coach pistols with silver mask butt caps. Flintlock officers' holster pistols and brass barrel flintlock blunderbusses with top spring bayonet. Also made Ferguson-type breech-loading rifles.

**Newton, Thomas** [about **1880**] Shop at Manchester, Lancashire. Made, over and under, metallic cartridge "express" rifles of .50 caliber.

**Nicholls, John** [**1730–1775**] Made flintlock holster pistols, brass mountings. Shop at Oxford. Name changed to **Thomas Nicholls** (probably son or nephew) 1775 to 1815.

**Nicholson, Edmund** [**1670–1710**] Shop in London. Made flintlock holster pistols and brass barrel flintlock blunderbusses.

**Nicholson, E. D.** [**1760–1808**] Shop in Cornhill, London. Made flintlock boxlock pocket pistols and officers' flintlock holster pistols. Cased pairs of flintlock duelling pistols with loading accessories. Also made flintlock carbines and muskets with Royal Cypher.

**Nidzer** [about **1830**] General gunsmith at Norwich, Norfolk.

**Nixon** [about **1830**] Shop at Birmingham. General gunsmith.

**Nock, Henry** [**1760–1810**] Famous English gunsmith with shops in London and Birmingham. One of the first gunmakers to use the sliding safety bar placed behind the hammer, locking the piece at half cock. In addition to the usual arms of flintlock pocket, and coach pistols, single and double barrel fowling pieces, and brass barrel blunderbusses, he made many special types of arms. For example, a seven-barrel flintlock "volley gun" with one hammer that fired all barrels at the same time. These were used for boarding in naval actions. Four-barrel and seven-barrel revolving flintlock pistols and carbines of the pepperbox type with one hammer and rotated by hand. Also heavy brass barrel swivel boat blunderbusses used by the Navy. Under Royal Government contract made flintlock carbines and muskets.

**Nock, Samuel** [1806–1860] Shop at 180 Fleet Street, London. Made flintlock fowling pieces and later percussion pepperboxes. Dealer and custom gunmaker.

**Noon** [about 1800] Made flintlock coach pistols. Shop at Burton-upon-Trent, Staffordshire.

**Norcott, John** [about 1630] One of seven London gunsmiths whose name appeared in the text of a commission granted by Charles I to make arms for the Crown.

**Norfolk** [about 1860] Shop at Bury St. Edmunds, Suffolk. General gunsmith.

**Norman, Benjamin** [about 1870] Custom gunmaker in London.

**Norris, Thomas** [about 1765] General gunsmith in Birmingham.

**North, E.** [1750–1775] Made screw barrel flintlock pocket pistols and flintlock carbines with the Royal Cypher. Shop in London.

**North, George** [1800–1830] Shop at Winchester, Hampshire. Made flintlock holster pistols.

**North, Thomas** [1830–1842] Made cased naval officers' percussion pistols. Shop at Southampton, Hampshire.

**Norton, Henry** [1820–1835] General gunsmith in London.

**Noyes, R.** [1800–1830] Shop at Warminster, Wiltshire. General gunsmith.

**Nunn & Son** [about 1850] Made cased double barrel, over and under, percussion traveling pistols with loading equipment. Shop in London.

**Nutt, William** [1680–1714] Did general gunsmithing in London.

**Nye, Nathaniel** [about 1650] Established a gunsmithery at Worcester.

# NOTES
## N

**Oakes, M.** [1758–1807] Made three-barrel boxlock flintlock pocket pistols with under spring bayonet and double barrel flintlock holster pistols. Also cased pairs of duelling pistols. Shop in London.

**Oates** [about 1780] Shop in London. General gunsmithing.

**Ogilvie** [about 1715] Established a gunsmithery in Scotland. Location not known.

**Oliver, H.** [about 1780] General gunsmith at Maidstone, Kent.

**Onion, John** [1770–1800] Shop at Birmingham. Made four-barrel flintlock pepperbox type of pistol, barrels rotated by hand. Name became **Onion & Simes** 1800 to 1804.

**Orr, Robert** [about 1675] Established a gunsmithery in Scotland. Location not known.

**Osborn** [about 1750] Shop in Pall Mall, London. Made flintlock holster pistols.

**Osborne & Co., Charles** [1858–1900] Shops in London and Birmingham. Made double barrel percussion pistols with top spring bayonet and percussion pepperboxes. Also double barrel percussion shotguns and percussion revolvers of Tranter Patent.

**Osborne, Henry** [1806–1830] General gunsmith in Birmingham.

**Osborne, John** [about 1770] Shop in Birmingham. General gunsmithing.

**Oughton, Joseph** [1767–1791] General gunsmith in Birmingham.

**Outridge, R.** [1793–1820] Made flintlock coach pistols. Shop in London.

**Oxborough** [about 1850] Shop at Woodbridge, Suffolk. General gunsmith.

## NOTES

O

**Page, T.** [1766–1776] Made cannon barrel boxlock flintlock pocket pistols and flintlock holster pistols. Shop at Norwich, Norfolk.

**Pagett** [about 1765] Shop in Birmingham. General gunsmithing.

**Paine, James** [about 1855] Custom gunmaker in London.

**Palmer** [about 1790] Made brass barrel blunderbuss type of flintlock pistol with under spring bayonet. Shop at Brighton, Sussex.

**Palmer, Joseph** [1760–1776] General gunsmith in Birmingham.

**Palmer, W.** [1680–1700] Made double barrel "turn over" flintlock fowling pieces. Shop in London.

**Palmer, William** [1790–1820] Shop at Rochester, Kent. Made cannon barrel boxlock flintlock pocket pistols and flintlock fowling pieces, also made four-barrel "duck foot" flintlock pistol. This pistol had the four barrels spread out like the fingers of the hand and had one hammer and one pan, the four barrels firing at one time.

**Palmer, William** [about 1810] General gunsmith in Birmingham.

**Panett** [about 1760] Shop at Salisbury, Wiltshire. General gunsmithing.

**Pape, W. R.** [1865–1890] Shop at Newcastle upon Tyne, Northumberland. Developed and patented a percussion chokebore shotgun. Also had percussion revolvers and later metallic cartridge revolvers.

**Parat** [about 1820] General gunsmith at Derby.

**Parke, W.** [about 1840] Under contract with the East India Company made cased traveling percussion pistols with loading equipment for service in India. Shop in London.

**Parker** [1800–1830] Shop at Bury St. Edmunds, Suffolk. Made boxlock flintlock pocket pistols.

**Parker, John** [about 1765] General gunsmithing in Birmingham.

**Parker, N.** [1812–1827] Shop in London. Made all metal Scottish-type flintlock pistols.

**Parker, William** [1790–1840] Shop in Holborn, London. He was the founder of a famous firm of gunmakers. Had the Royal Warrant. Made boxlock flintlock pocket pistols, flintlock holster pistols and brass barrel blunderbusses. Under Royal Government contract made flintlock musketoons. In 1829 when Sir Robert Peel organized the London Police, William Parker made flintlock and later percussion pistols for the Police organization. These were marked on the lock plate. "W. Parker Holborn" and on the barrel the Police Division to which they were issued, for example "Police Lambeth." The name was changed to **Parker, Field & Co.** 1840 to 1850 and located at 233 Holborn, London, and again changed to **Parker, Field & Sons** at above address 1850 to 1886. They made flintlock trade guns for the Hudson's Bay Company. Also boxlock percussion pocket pistols, cased naval officers' double barrel percussion pistols and double barrel percussion shotguns. Later made percussion pepperboxes and single-action .45 caliber percussion revolvers, Adams Patent.

**Parkes, John** [1767–1780] Made cannon barrel boxlock flintlock pocket pistols with silver mask butt caps and flintlock holster pistols. Shop in London.

**Parkhouse, Joseph** [1823–1840] Shop on High Street, Taunton, Somerset. Made percussion pocket pistols.

**Parkin, Thomas** [1825–1861] General gunsmith in London.

**Parkins, Thomas** [about 1645] Established a gunsmithery in London.

**Parkinson** [about 1860] Shop in Dublin, Ireland. Made double barrel, side-by-side, percussion holster pistols.

**Parkinson, Luke** [about 1830] General gunsmith at Boston, Lincolnshire.

**Parks** [about 1850] Custom gunmaker in London.

**Parr** [about 1810] Shop in Liverpool. General gunsmithing.

**Parr, I.** [1690–1740] Made Queen Anne–type flintlock coach pistols with silver mountings and flintlock duelling pistols. Shop in London.

**Parrett, R.** [about 1760] Shop at Salisbury, Wiltshire. General gunsmithing.

**Parry, F.** [about 1855] General gunsmith in London. He developed a handmade model of a .32 caliber percussion revolver. This was not patented.

**Parsons, Benjamin** [1813–1834] General gunsmith in Birmingham.

**Parsons, Gad & John** (son) [1810–1852] Shop in Birmingham. General gunsmiths.

**Parsons, T.** [1800–1845] Made flintlock pocket and holster pistols. Also flintlock fowling pieces. Later boxlock percussion pistols with spring bayonet and double barrel percussion sporting guns. Shop at Salisbury, Wiltshire.

**Parsons, W.** [about 1850] General gunsmith at Swaffham, Norfolk.

**Pasmore, John** [about 1640] Established a gunsmithery in London.

**Paterson, James** [1775–1800] Made all metal flintlock pistols with lobe-shaped butts. Shop in Edinburgh, Scotland.

**Paton & Sons, Edward** [1871–1885] Custom gunmakers in London.

**Paton & Walsh** [about 1860] Shop at Perth, Scotland. General gunsmiths.

**Patrick** [1780–1830] Made double barrel, over and under, flintlock pocket pistols and cased saw-handle flintlock duelling pistols of fine workmanship. Shop at Liverpool.

**Patrick** [1800–1820] Shop in Dublin, Ireland. Made flintlock coach pistols. These were cased with all accessories.

**Pattison, M. J.** [1800–1840] Under Royal Government contract made flintlock holster pistols and flintlock carbines. Also made for civilian trade double barrel flintlock fowling pieces. Shop in Dublin, Ireland.

**Pauly, Jean Samuel** [about 1815] General gunsmith in London.

**Payne, George** [about 1840] Shop on High Street, Taunton. General gunsmith.

**Peabody** [1869–1887] Custom gunmaker in London.

**Peacock, W.** [1820–1850] Shop on Duke Street, London. Made screw barrel boxlock flintlock pocket pistols and later double barrel percussion pistols.

**Peake, John** [1810–1830] General gunsmith in London.

**Pearsall, T.** [about 1750] Shop at Bury, Lancashire. Made four-barrel boxlock flintlock pocket pistols.

**Peddell, James** [1685–1714] Made flintlock Grenadiers' muskets with Royal Cypher. Shop in London.

**Peele, T.** [1720–1750] Shop at Whitehaven, Cumberland. Made flintlock holster pistols.

**Peevel, Joseph** [about 1875] Custom gunmaker in London.

**Pendrill, J.** [1800–1830] Made flintlock fowling pieces with silver mountings, of fine workmanship. Shop in Birmingham.

**Penn, John** [1867–1880] Custom gunmaker in London.

**Pennell** [about 1855] Shop in London. Made hammerless percussion pistols with belt hook.

**Pepper** [about 1820] Shop in Bedford. General gunsmithing.

**Pepper, G.** [about 1810] Made flintlock holster pistols with swivel ramrod. Shop in Dublin, Ireland.

**Perin, S. T.** [about 1830] General gunsmith at Windsor, Berkshire.

**Perkes, Thomas** [1882–1895] Custom gunmaker in London.

**Perkins, J.** [1810–1830] Made boxlock flintlock pocket pistols with folding trigger and brass barrel flintlock holster pistols. Shop in London.

**Perks, W.** [about 1790] Shop in London. Made flintlock coach and holster pistols.

**Perrins** [about 1850] Shop in Worcester. Made cased percussion pepperboxes with loading equipment. Used Birmingham Proof House.

**Perry, William** [about 1780] Made flintlock brass barrel pocket pistols and brass barrel flintlock blunderbusses. Shop in Birmingham.

**Petcairn, John** [about 1775] Shop at Edinburgh, Scotland. Made all metal flintlock pistols with scroll butts.

**Pether** [1815–1850] Made cased flintlock coach pistols and later percussion sporting guns. Shop at Oxford.

**Phelps** [about 1840] Shop at Marlborough, Wiltshire. Made double barrel percussion sporting guns.

**Philipps, H.** [1868–1886] Custom gunmakers in London.

**Philips, Thomas & Frank** [1714–1750] Made flintlock coach and holster pistols. Shop in London.

**Pickefatt, Charles** (2 generations) [1660–1750] Shop in London. Made screw barrel flintlock holster pistols with silver mask butt caps and flintlock coaching carbines.

**Pickfatt, Humphrey** [1714–1730] Made Queen Anne–type cannon barrel flintlock pistols. Shop in London.

**Pickford** [about 1690] Made flintlock carbines with Royal Cypher. Shop in London.

**Piercy, M.** [about 1830] Shop at New Malton, Yorkshire. General gunsmith.

**Piper, C.** [about 1770] Made flintlock coach pistols with lion mask butt caps. Shop in Windsor, Berkshire.

**Piper, C.** [1836–1850] Shop at Cambridge. Made percussion pepperboxes, cased naval officers' percussion pistols with belt hook, and cased pairs of percussion duelling pistols. Also percussion sporting rifles.

**Plant, Edward & Benjamin** [about 1815] General gunsmiths at Birmingham.

**Playfair, C.** [1810–1835] Shop at Aberdeen, Scotland. Made all metal, steel and silver, flintlock pistols. Later cased percussion traveling pistols, with swivel ramrods and loading equipment.

**Polinson** [1770–1790] General gunsmith in London. Developed a flint lock revolving cylinder pistol, hand rotated, which was a prototype of the Collier.

**Pollard, William** [1825–1840] Shop in London. General gunsmith.

**Porter** [about 1800] General gunsmith at Norwich, Norfolk.

**Porter, R.** [1770–1790] Made box-lock flintlock pocket pistols with folding trigger. Shop in London.

**Portlock, Godfrey** [about 1880] Custom gunmaker in London.

**Portlock, John** [about 1835] General gunsmith at Ripon, Yorkshire.

**Pottage, John** [about 1830] Shop in London. General gunsmithing.

**Pottage, Thomas** [about 1835] General gunsmith at Wakefield, Yorkshire.

**Potter, T.** [about 1840] General gunsmith in London.

**Potts, T. H.** [1840–1853] Shop at Haydon Square, London. Made percussion pocket pistols and percussion detachable dagger pistols. Under Royal Government contract made the Brunswick percussion rifle which was the first percussion arm used by the British Services. Also made brass barrel percussion naval pistols. Specialized in Presentation Pieces, a number of which were made for Indian princes. Name changed to **Potts & Hunt** 1853 to 1874.

**Powell** [1800–1830] Made brass barrel flintlock blunderbusses. Shop in Dublin, Ireland.

**Powell, Hugh & Stephen** [about 1715] General gunsmiths in London.

**Powell, James** [about 1775] Shop in London. General gunsmithing.

**Powell, Owen** [1850–1880] Shops in London and Sheffield. Made percussion pepperboxes and percussion revolvers, Adams Patent. Also double barrel percussion shotguns.

**Powell, William** [1815–1845] General gunsmith in Birmingham. Name changed to **William Powell & Son** 1845 to 1880. Made double barrel, over and under, percussion pistols with belt hooks and swivel ramrod. Later double barrel pin-fire sporting guns.

**Powers** [about 1780] Shop in London. General gunsmithing.

**Pratt, Isaac** [1770–1810] Made flintlock holster pistols. Shop on Throgmorten Street, London.

**Pratt, T.** [about 1830] General gunsmith at York.

**Predden** [about 1715] Shop in London. General gunsmithing.

**Press, Edward** [about 1800] Made flintlock holster pistols, with brass mounts. Shop at Bristol, Gloucestershire.

**Price** [about 1770] Shop at 227 Strand, London. General gunsmithing.

**Priest, Joseph** [about 1815] General gunsmith in Birmingham.

**Prince** [about 1835] Made percussion pocket pistols. Shop at Portsmouth, Hampshire.

**Prince, Frederick** [about 1875] Custom gunmaker and dealer at 138 Bond Street, London.

**Pringle, John** [about 1715] Shop in London. General gunsmithing.

**Pritchard, W.** [1835–1865] Shops in London and Birmingham. Made double barrel, over and under, percussion pistols with spring bayonet and cased percussion traveling pistols, also double barrel percussion sporting guns. An interesting piece made by Pritchard was a cased percussion ladies' "muff" pistol. This piece had an over-all length of 3.1 inches and .17 caliber. The case included a small metal powder flask and a bullet mold.

**Pritchett, Samuel** [1810–1825] General gunsmith in London. Name changed to **Richard Pritchett** (probably son or nephew) 1825 to 1864. Under Royal Government contract made percussion muskets and musketoons.

**Probin, Charles** [1770–1812] Made boxlock flintlock pocket pistols with folding trigger and cased duelling pistols with loading accessories; both of fine workmanship. Shop at Hull, Yorkshire.

**Probin, Thomas** (2 generations) [1700–1780] Shop in London. Made flintlock duelling and holster pistols. Also flintlock fowling pieces.

**Probyn, John F.** [1780–1831] Under Royal Government contract made flintlock holster pistols, and flintlock rifles and carbines. Shop in London.

**Proctor, William** [about 1845] General gunsmith in London.

**Prosser, John** [1770–1820] Shop at Charing Cross, London. Made boxlock flintlock pistols and officers' flintlock dragoon pistols.

**Prosser, W.** [about 1835] Made percussion holster pistols. Shop in Gloucester.

**Prudie, Henry** [about 1880] Custom gunmaker in London.

**Pryde, Alexander** [about 1595] Established a gunsmithery at St. Andrews, Scotland.

**Pryse & Co., Charles & John** [1840–1888] General gunsmiths in London. In November 1876, Charles Pryse patented a .45 caliber "break open" or "tip down" metallic cartridge revolver with barrel latch. This patent was sold to Philip Webley & Son.

**Puckle, James** [about 1720] Shop in London. General gunsmithing.

**Pulman** [about 1840] Shop at Axminster, Devonshire. Made cased percussion duelling pistols with loading accessories.

**Purcell, Benjamin** [about 1830] General gunsmith at Richmond, Surrey.

**Purdey, James** [1816–1868] Founder of a famous firm of gunmakers. Shop at 314 Oxford Street, London. Made double barrel flintlock fowling pieces, later percussion pocket and holster pistols. Also made six-barrel "turn over" percussion pocket pistols and double barrel percussion shotguns and rifles. Name changed to **James Purdey & Sons** 1868 to 1900, located at Audley House, South Audley Street, London. Made double barrel .45 caliber metallic cartridge "express" rifle.

**Pye** [about 1785] Shop at Ross, Herefordshire. General gunsmithing.

NOTES
P

**Radoe, Henry** [about **1590**] Established a gunsmithery at Norwich, Norfolk.

**Ransford, M.** [**1710–1750**] Made flintlock holster pistols with silver mountings. Shop at Dublin, Ireland.

**Raper, Benjamin** [about **1830**] General gunsmith at Leeds, Yorkshire.

**Ravens, J.** [about **1815**] Shop at Birmingham. General gunsmith.

**Rawlins, John** [about **1835**] General gunsmith at Birmingham.

**Rawson** [**1750–1790**] Shop at Norwich, Norfolk. Made flintlock holster pistols.

**Rea, John** [**1782–1830**] Made flintlock pocket pistols. Under contract for the East India Company made flintlock holster pistols and heavy wall pivot flintlock guns. Shop in London.

**Rea, Thomas** [**1790–1820**] Made screw barrel flintlock pocket pistols and flintlock holster pistols. Shop in London.

**Read** [about **1800**] Shop at Portsmouth, Southampton. Made double barrel, over and under, boxlock flintlock pocket pistols.

**Real** [about **1840**] Made boxlock percussion pistols. Shop at Dundee, Scotland.

**Recktor** [about **1650**] Established a gunsmithery at Broughton, Lancashire.

**Reddell** [**1760–1812**] General gunsmith in London.

**Reddish, J.** [about **1850**] Made double barrel percussion sporting guns. Shop in London.

**Redfern, Bartholomew** [**1790–1836**] Shop in Birmingham. Made cannon brass barrel flintlock pocket pistols and flintlock holster pistols with brass mountings. Also brass barrel flintlock blunderbusses. Name changed to **Redfern & Bourne** 1836 to 1860. Made percussion pepperboxes and double barrel percussion sporting guns.

**Reed** [about **1800**] Shop at Aylsham, Norfolk. Made flintlock holster pistols.

**Reed, Archibald** [**1850–1868**] Made cased percussion traveling pistols and percussion shotguns. Shop in London.

**Reed, George** [**1700–1720**] Shop in London. General gunsmithing.

**Reed, J.** [**1700–1740**] Shop in London. Used "Londini" in marking his pieces. Made Queen Anne–type flintlock pocket pistols and flintlock duelling pistols with silver mountings.

**Reeve & Graves** [**1760–1810**] Made flintlock pocket pistols and under Royal Government contract made flintlock holster pistols. Shops in London and Birmingham.

**Reeve, William** [about **1830**] General gunsmith at Yarmouth, Norfolk.

**Reeves, C.** [about **1810**] Shop in Birmingham. Made boxlock flintlock pocket pistols with folding trigger and spring bayonet.

**Reeves, Charles** [about **1860**] Custom gunmaker in London.

**Reid** [about **1840**] Made cased percussion traveling pistols with loading equipment. Shop in London.

**Reilly** [about **1860**] Shop at 316 Holborn, London. Made boxlock percussion pocket pistols with folding trigger, cased percussion pepperboxes and percussion revolvers, Adams Patent.

**Reilly & Co., Edward M.** [**1850–1898**] Shop on Oxford Street, London. Made double barrel, over and under, percussion pistols with cap box in

D

butt plate, and cased percussion duelling pistols. Also percussion pepperboxes.

**Reilly, Joseph Charles** [1830–1858] Made percussion traveling pistols with swivel ramrod and cased percussion pepperboxes with loading accessories. Shop in London.

**Restel** [1855–1865] Custom gunmaker in London.

**Reule, John** [about 1630] Established a gunsmithery in Scotland. Location not known.

**Reynolds & Forbes** [about 1790] General gunsmiths in London.

**Reynolds, Thomas** [1790–1830] Shop in Coventry, Warwickshire. Made flintlock pocket pistols with folding trigger, and flintlock duelling pistols with gold ventholes. Also double barrel flintlock fowling pieces.

**Rhoades, C. T.** [about 1850] Shop at Salisbury, Wiltshire. Made boxlock, percussion pocket pistols with folding triggers and percussion sporting guns.

**Rice, George** [about 1760] Shop in London. General gunsmithing.

**Rich & Hollis** [about 1840] General gunsmiths in London.

**Richards** [about 1820] Shop at Cork, Ireland. General gunsmithing.

**Richards, Henry** [about 1750] Shop in Blackfriars Road, London. Made brass barrel flintlock blunderbusses.

**Richards, J.** [about 1840] General gunsmith at Hunts Court, Taunton, Somerset.

**Richards, John** (2 generations) [1745–1810] Shops in Strand, London, and Birmingham. Under Royal Government contract made screw barrel flintlock pocket pistols for the Inland Revenue Services. These were marked on the barrel "I.R.S.," also made flintlock holster pistols for this Service. For civilian sale made cannon barrel Queen Anne–type of flintlock pocket pistols and cased flintlock traveling and duelling pistols. Also bell muzzle flintlock pistols with under spring bayonet.

**Richards, Joseph** [1800–1818] Shop at New Street, Birmingham. General gunsmith.

**Richards, Theophilus** [1790–1830] Shops in London and on High Street, Birmingham. Made flintlock coach and duelling pistols with silver mountings, and brass barrel flintlock blunderbusses with top spring bayonet. Under Royal Government contract made flintlock muskets.

**Richards, Thomas** [1750–1780] Shop in London. Made cannon barrel boxlock flintlock pocket pistols and under Royal Government contract made flintlock holster pistols. The pair of Captain William Delaplace's (Commandant at Fort Ticonderoga) brass barrel flintlock pistols captured by Ethan Allen are marked "T. Richards London 1773."

**Richards, William Westley & Westley** (son) [1812–1872] William Westley Richards was born in Birmingham, England in 1788 of a family of merchants and silversmiths. In 1812 he established a gunsmith shop at 82 High Street, Birmingham, selecting his gunsmiths from the already thriving gun trade in Birmingham. His first production was high-grade flintlock fowling pieces. In 1813 he was an active petitioner in establishing the Birmingham Proof House through an act of Parliament.

He had the foresight to realize that he had to have a London outlet for his firearms, as the London market was by far the largest, and also for possible export trade to the Continent.

He chose the most fashionable quarter of London, a street made famous as the resort of the luxury class to which his guns appealed. The establishment was opened in 1815 at the then numbered 170 Bond Street. He selected as his agent in London, William Bishop, a Londoner well known in the gun and shooting fields and who became known as "the Bishop of Bond Street."

Encountering daily members of the world of fashion and sport, he was not long in becoming a personal adviser to them. The young bloods, officers of the Army and Navy, fashionable county squires could always find a rendezvous at Westley Richards on Bond Street, and it was a delight to banter wit with "the Bishop."

William Bishop was enormous in size and noted for his immaculate dress, which was always the same any hour of the day—a broad-brimmed topper, a white tie, a swallow-tailed coat, a white apron to his ankles, and shirt sleeves turned over the forearm like the cuff of a high church dignitary. He contributed much to the success and sales of Westley Richards firearms. Bishop died in 1871 after fifty-six years in the Bond Street establishment and was regarded by the generations he knew with esteem and affection and to many he was their mentor of the noble art of shooting.

In 1821 William Westley Richards took out his first patents for percussion lock improvements on gun and pistol locks. The change from the flintlock to the detonating system was then gradually being effected, and Richards was one of the first Birmingham gunmakers to obtain a license from Forsyth for the manufacture of his patented percussion primer. The early metallic caps had a tendency to break into fragments at the time of discharge with bad results to whomever was firing the piece. Richards' new design of nipple and cover for the primer plus a new pattern of cap overcame this. Richards was also one of the first to use tin foil inside the cap to protect the detonating charge.

The following is from a printed label on a box of 500 primers and dated 1836: "The waterproof safety primers invented by Westley Richards—for prevention of accident by the escape of unexploded material or copper. The shortening of the distance to the charge and the inconvenience of the touchhole ever being liable to stop up. These primers are certain to fire in damp or bad weather. They possess the advantage of being made doubly secure if the sportsman is determined to shoot in hard driving rain. Melt a little white or beeswax and lightly dip the open end of the primers in the liquid, it will so seal the touchhole when the primer is applied that the gun may be fired under water. This should only be resorted to when absolutely necessary, as the primers in their present state effectually resist as much wet as the sportsman likes to encounter."

Other inventions followed which related to different branches of gunnery, such as projectiles, revolvers, and rifles. In 1834 Richards introduced the first "flip-up tangent gunsight" to be used in the British Army. In 1840 he received the Royal Warrant and appointment as Gunmaker to H.R.H., the Prince Consort, and Richards was granted a special Medal Award for his display at the London Exhibition at the Crystal Palace in 1851.

Westley Richards, eldest son of William Westley Richards, born August 8, 1814, succeeded his father as active head of the business in 1855, when it became **Westley Richards & Company.** He expanded the business on a more international scope in accord with the trend at that time of British Government in exports. From 1859 to 1868 he perfected the falling block breech-loading rifle, which was the forerunner of the British Martini Service Arm, and the Government paid £45,000 in royalties for the falling block patents. From 1866 to 1872 he developed the solid-drawn metallic cartridge case and set up new forms and sizes of cartridges. This involved the design for given purposes, the shape of the cartridge, the weight of the bullet, and the powder capacity of the case. Richards succeeded in building up a complete series of cartridges, which proved to be of worldwide utility, and the Westley Richards' No. 1 carbine cartridge could be purchased anywhere in the world.

The history of the Westley Richards firm shown by the records of the Crown Patent Office shows twenty-two patents in gunmaking in its various phases, every one of them successful and of practical value to the firearms industry. Westley Richards was closely associated with Sir Joseph Whitworth and produced the first rifles with the Whitworth type of rifling.

Richards retired from the business in 1872 and died May 27, 1897, in his 83rd year. Westley Richards left his mark on every branch of the industry and did much for the practical advancement of gunmaking of his time.

**Richardson** [about 1850] Shop in Limerick, Ireland. Made cased percussion traveling pistols with loading equipment. Also percussion revolvers, Adams Patent.

**Richardson** [1820–1850] Shop at Winchester, Southampton. Made boxlock percussion pocket pistols.

**Richardson** [1790–1830] Shops at London and Manchester, Lancashire. Made boxlock flintlock pocket pistols and later percussion rifled pistols with belt hooks, and percussion holster pistols.

**Richardson, J.** [about 1820] General gunsmith in Birmingham.

**Ridley, Thomas** [1810–1860] Shop in London. General gunsmith.

**Ridley, William** [1812–1832] General gunsmith in London.

**Rigby, John** [1867–1890] Shops in London and Dublin, Ireland. Made double barrel, over and under, percussion pistols with belt hooks and brass barrel, bell muzzle, percussion pistols. Also .44 caliber percussion revolvers. Name changed to **John Rigby & Co., Ltd.**, at 43 Sackville Street, London, and plant at 5 Crown Yard, Stanhope Street, London, 1890 to 1900. Dealers and custom gunmakers, made breech-loading sporting guns with Bacon's Patent action.

**Rigby, William** [1827–1867] Shop at 24 Suffolk Street, Dublin, Ireland. Made brass barrel flintlock blunderbusses for the Irish Royal Mail Service. Also made pepperbox type of four-barrel carbine with one hammer, and double barrel percussion shotguns.

**Riley, William S.** [1874–1887] General gunsmith in Birmingham.

**Rimes, J.** [about 1800] Made flintlock coach pistols. Shop in London.

**Rippingile, E.** [about 1850] Custom gunmaker in London.

**Rivière, Isaac** [1815–1841] Shop in London. Made flintlock pocket pistols, silver mounted, of fine design and workmanship. Later made cased percussion duelling pistols with loading equipment. Name changed to **Henry Rivière** (probably son or nephew) 1841 to 1867. Made naval officers' percussion pistols with belt hooks and double-action percussion pepperboxes.

**Robb, Andrew** [about 1820] Shop in Aberdeen, Scotland. General gunsmithing.

**Robbins, C.** [1830–1850] General gunsmith in London.

**Roberts, George** [about 1860] Shop in London. General gunsmith.

**Roberts, John S.** [1852–1868] Made percussion pocket pistols and breech-loading percussion rifles. Shop in Birmingham.

**Robertson, J.** [1840–1851] Shop at Haddington, East Lothian County, Scotland. Made percussion pocket pistols with folding triggers.

**Robertson, John** [about 1870] Custom gunmaker in London.

**Robin, J.** [about 1750] Made cannon barrel flintlock coach pistols with silver mask butt caps. Shop in London.

**Robinson** [about 1770] Shop in Bristol, Gloucestershire. General gunsmithing.

**Robinson** [about 1790] Made flintlock coach pistols with silver mountings, and brass barrel flintlock blunderbusses. Shop in London.

**Robinson, A.** [about 1850] Shop in London. Made boxlock percussion pocket pistols with folding triggers.

**Robinson, John** [1810–1832] Made screw barrel boxlock flintlock pocket pistols with folding triggers. Shop in Liverpool.

**Rock, Denis T.** [about 1870] Custom gunmaker in London.

**Rodda, R. B.** [about 1840] Shops in London and Calcutta, India. Made cased percussion belt pistols with loading equipment.

**Rogers, James** [about 1850] Shop at Sheffield, Yorkshire. Made percussion detachable dagger pistols with receptacle in butt for caps and balls. Also naval percussion pistols with spring bayonet.

**Rolfe, W. J.** [about 1810] General gunsmith in Birmingham.

**Ronalds** [about 1800] Made cased flintlock duelling pistols with silver mounts. Shop in Canterbury, Kent.

**Rooke, W. & S.** [1770–1820] Under Royal Government contract made flintlock holster pistols with swivel ramrods, also cased flintlock coach pistols. Shop in London.

**Rose, James** [about 1810] General gunsmith in Birmingham.

**Rose, William** [about 1715] Shop in London. General gunsmithing.

**Ross** [about 1830] General gunsmith at Dover, Kent.

**Ross** [about 1810] Shop at Edinburgh, Scotland. Made double barrel flintlock fowling pieces.

**Rosson, Charles** [about 1840] Made transition-type percussion revolver with top hammer. Shop in London.

**Rowland, G.** [about 1830] Shop in London. General gunsmithing.

**Rowland, Henry** [about 1630] One of seven London gunsmiths whose name appeared in a commission granted by Charles I to make Royal arms.

**Rowland, J.** [about 1705] Established a gunsmithery in London.

**Rowland, R.** [1680–1718] Made brass mounted flintlock holster pistols. Shop in London.

**Rowntree, James** [1810–1840] General gunsmith at Barnard Castle, Durham. Attributed to have made a percussion fowling piece for Joshua Shaw, using steel caps.

**Rubans, C.** [about 1800] General gunsmith in London.

**Rutter, William** [about 1860] Custom gunmaker in London.

**Ryan, G.** [about **1800**] Shop in Dublin, Ireland. General gunsmithing.

**Ryan, S.** [about **1700**] Established a gunsmithery at Manchester, Lancashire.

**Ryan & Watson** [1765–1835] Shops at London and Birmingham. Made cannon barrel boxlock flintlock pocket pistols with spring bayonet, and screw barrel boxlock coach pistols; also double barrel flintlock fowling pieces.

**Ryding** [about **1780**] General gunsmith in London.

**Rylands & Darby** [about **1810**] Made flintlock sporting rifles and fowling pieces. Shop in London.

NOTES

R

**Sadleir, F.** [1770–1785] Shop in London. General gunsmithing.

**Sale, Edward** [about 1710] Established a gunsmithery in London.

**Salmon** [about 1800] Made double barrel flintlock pistols. Shop in London.

**Sandwell, Stephen** [1770–1780] General gunsmith in London.

**Saunders, Theodore** [1699–1714] Made brass barrel, bell muzzle, flintlock pistols. Shop in London.

**Saunson, J.** [1750–1800] Shop in London. Made flintlock pocket pistols and flintlock holster pistols with swivel ramrod.

**Scarlet, D.** [about 1830] Shop at Swaffham, Norfolk. General gunsmithing.

**Schlesinger, Joseph** [about 1860] Custom gunmaker in London.

**Schulte, Charles** [about 1870] Custom gunmaker in London.

**Scott, Andrew** [about 1725] Made all metal flintlock pistols, with heart-shaped butts. Shop in Edinburgh, Scotland.

**Scott, D.** [1727–1745] Shop in Edinburgh, Scotland (used the spelling "Edinboro" on his pieces). Made cannon screw barrel, Queen Anne–type flintlock holster pistols.

**Scott, James** [1752–1790] Made flintlock holster pistols with walnut stocks. Shop in Edinburgh, Scotland.

**Scott, R.** [about 1850] Made cased percussion traveling pistols with loading accessories and naval percussion pistols with belt hook. Shop in London.

**Scott, W. & C.** [1834–1858] Shops in London and Birmingham. Made a wide range of percussion small and long arms featuring double barrel percussion shotguns. Name changed to **W. & C. Scott & Son** 1858 to 1897, when they merged with Philip Webley & Son to become **Webley & Scott Revolver & Arms Co., Ltd.**

**Scott, Walter** [about 1870] Custom gunmaker in Edinburgh, Scotland.

**Scott, William** [about 1855] Shop in London. General gunsmith.

**Scudamore** [about 1750] Made flintlock pocket and coach pistols also cased pairs of flintlock duelling pistols with all accessories. Shop in London.

**Searle, Thomas** [about 1870] Custom gunmaker in London.

**Seddon, James** [about 1850] General gunsmith in London.

**"Segallas" or "Segalas"** [1720–1800] This was a type of flintlock pistol, mostly pocket size, which appeared for sale in England with the forged word "London" or "A Londres" on the lock plate or barrel. These were made mostly in France or Belgium. They were of inferior quality and workmanship but highly ornamental.

**Segar** [1780–1800] General gunsmith in London.

**Shambles, George** [about 1830] Shop in Barnsley, Yorkshire. General gunsmith.

**Sharman** [about 1820] General gunsmith at Peterborough, Northampton.

**Sharp** [1750–1810] Made brass barrel flintlock blunderbusses. Shop at Maidstone, Kent.

**Sharp, John** [about 1815] Shop in Birmingham. Made double barrel boxlock flintlock pocket pistols.

**Sharp & Pitt** [1750–1800] Made double barrel, over and under, flintlock holster pistols. Shop in London.

**Sharp, William** [1835–1856] Shop in London. Made percussion holster pistols.

**Sharpe** [1800–1840] Made brass barrel flintlock holster pistols and later boxlock percussion pocket pistols with folding trigger. Shop in London.

**Shaw & Crane** [about 1780] Shop in London. Made flintlock fowling pieces.

**Shaw, John** [about 1680] Established a gunsmithery in London.

**Shaw, William** [about 1830] Shop at Manchester, Lancashire. General gunsmithing.

**Shields, John** [1750–1775] Made all metal flintlock pistols with scroll butts. Shop at Stirling, Scotland.

**Shelton** [about 1655] General gunsmithing. His address was known as the "Sign of the Crossed Guns," Covent Garden, London.

**Shepard** [about 1800] Shop at Uxbridge, Middlesex. General gunsmithing.

**Shepherd, W.** [about 1770] General gunsmith at Canterbury, Kent.

**Sheppard, John** [1770–1817] Made cannon barrel Queen Anne–type flintlock pocket pistols. Shop in London.

**Sherwood** [about 1850] Shop at Portsmouth, Hampshire. Made naval officers' percussion pistols with belt hook.

**Sherwood, J. W.** [1800–1835] General gunsmith in London.

**Shiel, John** [about 1775] Shop in Edinburgh, Scotland. Made all metal flintlock pistols with scroll butts.

**Shires, Alexander** [about 1700] Made all metal flintlock pistols with heart-shaped butt. Shop in Old Meldrum, Scotland.

**Shirls** [about 1795] Shop in London. General gunsmithing.

**Shorey, Joseph** [about 1750] Shop in London (used "Londini" in marking his pieces). Made flintlock pocket pistols.

**Showell, C.** [about 1830] General gunsmith at Sheffield, Yorkshire.

**Sibley, John** [1714–1750] Made Queen Anne–type flintlock holster pistols, and large bore boat swivel fowling pieces. Shop in London.

**Sibthorpe, Robert** [about 1715] Shop in London. General gunsmithing.

**Siddall, W.** [about 1830] General gunsmith at Chester.

**Siddons** [about 1840] Made percussion rifles, Blisset Patent. Shop in London.

**Silk, John** [about 1790] Shop in London. Made steel barrel blunderbusses.

**Simkin, Benjamin** [about 1830] General gunsmith at St. Helens, Lancashire.

**Simkin, Thomas** [about 1835] Shop at Bolton, Lancashire. General gunsmithing.

**Simmons** [about 1850] Made naval percussion pistols where the trigger guard had a belt hook extension. Shop in London.

**Simmonds, Joseph** [1802–1845] Made flintlock fowling pieces and later double barrel percussion pistols (double barrels bored from one piece of steel). Shop in Birmingham.

**Simpson, John** [about 1695] Established a gunsmithery at Edinburgh, Scotland.

**Simpson, W.** [1689–1715] General gunsmith in London.

Sims, John [about 1765] Shop in Birmingham. General gunsmithing.

Sinckler, Richard [1700–1720] General gunsmith in London.

Sinderby [about 1785] Shop in London. General gunsmith.

Sitlington, William [about 1745] Made screw barrel flintlock coach pistols with silver mask butt caps. Shop in London.

Skinner, John [1650–1670] (Brother of Thomas) Shop at Tower Hill, London. Made flintlock pistols, carbines, and blunderbusses.

Skinner, Thomas [1654–1665] Shop in Leadenhall Street, London. Supplied the army in 1654 with "100 pairs of pistols and 20 carbines"; also made brass barrel flintlock blunderbusses.

Slingsby [about 1860] Made percussion sporting rifles. Shop at Retford, Nottinghamshire.

Smart, Francis [about 1715] Shop in London. General gunsmithing.

Smart, John [1690–1720] Shop in London (used the spelling "Londini" to mark his pieces). Made flintlock fowling pieces.

Smart, W. [about 1830] General gunsmith at Gloucester.

Smith [1830–1850] Shop at Braintree, Essex. Made double barrel, over and under, percussion pistols with folding triggers.

Smith [about 1585] Established a gunsmithery at St. Andrews, Scotland.

Smith, Charles T. [1825–1850] Made double barrel "turn over" percussion pistols, and cased percussion duelling pistols with loading equipment. Shop in London.

Smith, Edwin [1850–1870] Shop in London. Made boxlock percussion pocket pistols.

Smith & Co., F. I. [1810–1850] Made double barrel flintlock pocket pistols with two hammers and two triggers and, later, percussion transition-type revolvers. Shop in Birmingham.

Smith, George [about 1820] Shop at Newcastle under Lyme, Staffordshire. Made brass barrel flintlock coach pistols.

Smith, George [1859–1897] Made double barrel percussion shotguns. Shop in London.

Smith, Gulielmus (William) [1672–1686] Gunsmithery at Bellachastel (now Castle Grant) Scotland. Made snaphaunce guns.

Smith, H. [1825–1840] Made percussion pocket pistols with folding triggers. His early percussion pistols had a patented "cap holder." Shop in London.

Smith, H. E. [about 1835] General gunsmith at Sheffield, Yorkshire.

Smith, Isaac [1747–1790] Made double barrel boxlock flintlock pocket pistols and screw barrel Queen Anne–type flintlock coach pistols. Shop in London.

Smith, John [1840–1860] Shop at 28 Loverday Street, Birmingham. Had Royal Government contract for percussion revolvers.

Smith, Joshua [1730–1750] Made flintlock holster pistols and flintlock fowling pieces. Shop in London.

Smith, Michael [1815–1826] General gunsmith in Birmingham.

Smith, Orlando [about 1860] Dealer and shop at Derby. Made cased percussion revolvers, Adams Patent, with all accessories.

Smith, R. [1800–1830] Made brass barrel flintlock blunderbusses. Shop at Uttoxeter, Staffordshire.

**Smith, Samuel & Charles** (son) [1849–1875] Shop at 64 Princes Street, Leicester Square, London. Made double barrel percussion sporting guns and pill-lock officers' holster pistols.

**Smith, T.** [about 1830] General gunsmith at Leek, Staffordshire.

**Smith, Thomas** [about 1850] Made double barrel percussion holster pistols. Shop in London.

**Smith & Townsend** [about 1860] Shop in Birmingham. Made double-action percussion revolvers.

**Smith, William** [1810–1845] Made flintlock coach pistols. Later made double barrel tube-lock sporting guns of G. Moore Patent. Shop at Leicester Square, London.

**Smithett, George** [about 1715] Shop in London. General gunsmithing.

**Smyth, Robert** [about 1630] Established a gunsmithery in Scotland. Location not known.

**Snowdon, George** [about 1835] Shop at Alnwick, Northumberland. General gunsmith.

**Snowill, H.** [about 1850] Shop at Inverness, Scotland. Made cased double barrel percussion sporting guns with loading and cleaning equipment.

**Southall** [1800–1845] Made brass barrel boxlock pocket and coach pistols and flintlock holster pistols. Later made rifled barrel percussion pocket pistols and transition percussion revolvers. Shop in London.

**Southall, John** [1770–1817] Under contract with the East India Company, made brass barrel flintlock blunderbusses. Shop in Birmingham.

**Southall & Co., Richard** [about 1850] Made percussion pepperboxes. Shop in Birmingham.

**Southwell, William** [1836–1870] General gunsmith in London.

**Sowery, J.** [about 1730] Made screw barrel Queen Anne–type flintlock coach pistols with silver mask butt caps. Shop in London.

**Sowery, William** [about 1715] Established a gunsmithery in London.

**Spearman, J.** [about 1795] General gunsmith in London.

**Spearman, T.** [1850–1864] Custom gunmaker in London.

**Spencer** [about 1800] Shop at Kings Lynn, Norfolk. General gunsmithing.

**Spencer** [about 1820] Shop in London. Made boxlock flintlock pocket pistols with folding triggers and cased flintlock coach pistols of fine workmanship. Also brass barrel flintlock blunderbusses with top spring bayonet.

**Spencer, Charles & John** [about 1815] Made flintlock fowling pieces. Shop in Birmingham.

**Spencer, M. S.** [about 1830] Shop at Lyme Regis, Dorsetshire. General gunsmithing.

**Spies, A.** [about 1780] General gunsmith in London.

**Spurling** [1810–1835] Made cased flintlock duelling pistols with loading accessories. Shop in London.

**Squire, W.** [1777–1800] Shop in London. Made flintlock fowling pieces.

**Squires, James** [1860–1892] Shop in London. Made percussion revolvers, Tranter Patent, and later metallic cartridge rifles, Snider Patent.

**Squires, T.** [1800–1820] Made flintlock fowling pieces and rifles. Shop in London.

**Stace, Joseph** [about 1680] Shop in London. General gunsmithing.

**Stacy** [about 1840] Made boxlock percussion pocket pistols with folding triggers. Shop in Sheffield, Yorkshire.

**Stanley** [about 1825] General gunsmith in London.

**Stanton** [about 1580] Established a gunsmithery in London.

**Stanton** [1750–1778] Made brass barrel flintlock holster pistols with silver mask butt caps. Shop in London.

**Stanton** [about 1870] Custom gunmaker at Wolverhampton, Staffordshire.

**Stanton & Son** [about 1850] General gunsmiths at Chester.

**Stanton, S.** [about 1835] Shop at Shrewsbury, Shropshire. General gunsmith.

**Staples, William** [1752–1770] Made iron barrel flintlock blunderbusses with top spring bayonet. Shop in Birmingham.

**Stapp, Richard** [about 1855] Custom gunmaker in London.

**Starnes** [about 1800] Shop at Romford, Essex. General gunsmith.

**Staton** [1750–1790] Made flintlock holster pistols. Shop in London.

**Staudenmayer, S.** [1790–1830] Shop in London. Made double barrel, over and under, flintlock pocket pistols.

**Stephen, R.** [about 1785] Made flintlock coach and dragoon pistols. Shop at Bristol, Gloucestershire.

**Stephens, J.** [1790–1820] Shop at Queen Street, Byranston Square, London. Made detachable dagger flintlock pocket pistols and cased silver mounted flintlock duelling pistols of fine workmanship.

**Steuart, Daniel** [about 1690] Made all metal flintlock (dog-lock) pistols with scroll butt. Shop at Perth, Scotland.

**Stevens, James & Thomas** [1810–1852] Made cased flintlock coach pistols with loading accessories. Later made cased duelling pistols, and under Royal Government contract made percussion carbines. Shop in London.

**Stewart, P.** [1861–1871] Custom gunmaker in London.

**Stirling, John** [about 1850] Shop at Burnley, Lancashire. Made cased percussion sporting guns with loading and cleaning equipment.

**Stocker, S. W.** [about 1835] General gunsmith at Bristol, Gloucestershire.

**Stocker, T.** [about 1830] Shop at Yeovil, Somerset. General gunsmithing.

**Stokes, Thomas** [about 1850] Made officers' percussion holster pistols. Shop in Birmingham.

**Stoneman, J.** [about 1660] Established a gunsmithery in London.

**Stones, M.** [about 1700] Made flintlock holster pistols. Shop in London.

**Storer, David** [about 1850] General gunsmith in London.

**Storms, B. C.** [about 1865] Custom gunmaker in London.

**Strachan, Andrew** [1700–1730] Shop at Edzell, Perthshire, Scotland. Made all metal flintlock pistols with heart-shaped butts.

**Strickland** [about 1800] Made flintlock holster pistols. Shop at Uxbridge, Middlesex.

**Stringer, Ralph** [1714–1750] Made brass barrel, bell muzzle, flintlock coach pistols. Shop in London.

**Stringer, William** [1850–1868] Custom gunmaker in London.

**Struman, Benjamin** [about 1850] General gunsmith in London.

**Stuart, John** [1701–1750] Made all metal flintlock pistols with heart-shaped butts. Shop in Edinburgh, Scotland.

**Stubing, William** [about 1835] General gunsmith at Blackburn, Lancashire.

**Sturman, George** [1800–1830] Shop at Islington, London. Made flintlock fowling pieces and was active until 1830. His two sons, Philip and William George, carried on the business from 1830 to 1850. Made percussion holster pistols.

**Styan, Thomas** [1815–1835] Made boxlock flintlock pocket pistols with folding triggers, and brass barrel blunderbuss type of flintlock pistols. Shop at Manchester, Lancashire.

**Such** [about 1800] Shop at Worcester. General gunsmithing.

**Such, Joseph** [about 1820] General gunsmith at Birmingham.

**Sutherland, James** [about 1790] Made all metal flintlock pistols with scroll butts. Shop in Edinburgh, Scotland.

**Sutherland, R.** [1790–1827] Shops in London and Birmingham. Made double barrel flintlock pocket pistols, and cased flintlock coach and duelling pistols of fine workmanship. Also flintlock fowling pieces.

**Swallow** [about 1750] Made double barrel flintlock pocket pistols. Shop in London.

**Swinburne & Son, C. B.** [1846–1862] Under Royal Government contract made percussion carbines. Shop in Birmingham.

**Sykes** [1800–1830] Made boxlock flintlock pocket pistols, and double barrel flintlock holster pistols with detachable carbine stock. Shop in Oxford.

**Sykes, Thomas** [about 1794] Shop in London. General gunsmithing.

**Sylven, T.** [1864–1880] Custom gunmaker in London.

# NOTES

S

**Tambeur, Bernard** [about 1865] Custom gunmaker in London.

**Tanner & Co., F.** [1850–1880] Made breech-loading percussion holster pistols and under contract made percussion rifles for the Russian Government. Shop in London.

**Tanner, L.** [1745–1795] Shop in London. General gunsmithing.

**Tarles, J.** [about 1660] Established a gunsmithery in London.

**Tarratt, J.** [about 1850] Made percussion pistols with swivel ramrod and belt hook. Shop in London.

**Tate, B.** [about 1830] General gunsmith in London.

**Tate & Lill** [about 1800] Shop in Louth, Lincolnshire. General gunsmithing.

**Tatham & Egg** [1760–1800] Shop at 37 Charing Cross, London. Made cased flintlock duelling pistols with loading accessories and double barrel flintlock fowling pieces all of fine workmanship. Name changed to **Henry Tatham** (2 generations) at the above address 1800 to 1865. Under Royal Government contract made flintlock carbines and later naval percussion pistols with belt hooks. For civilian use made percussion pepperboxes and percussion sporting rifles. Henry Tatham made flintlock rifles up to 1865 for Royal presentation to Canadian Indian chiefs; these rifles had a plaque of Queen Victoria and the Royal Arms.

**Tayler & Mander** [1780–1810] Made double barrel, over and under, flintlock coach pistols, and, under Royal Government contract, naval flintlock pistols with belt hooks. Shop in Birmingham.

**Taylor** [1750–1800] Made cannon barrel, boxlock flintlock coach pistols with silver mask butt caps. Shop in London.

**Taylor, Edward** [1767–1786] General gunsmith in Birmingham

**Taylor, G.** [about 1680] Made brass barrel flintlock holster pistols. Shop in London.

**Taylor, J. & S.** [about 1815] General gunsmiths in Birmingham.

**Taylor, William** [about 1840] Made percussion pocket pistols. Shop in Beverley, Yorkshire.

**Templeman** [about 1790] Shop at Salisbury, Wiltshire. General gunsmithing.

**Teray** [about 1790] General gunsmith in Dublin, Ireland.

**Terry** [about 1855] General gunsmith in London.

**Thomas** [1776–1790] Shop in Birmingham. General gunsmithing.

**Thomas, L.** [1760–1810] Made three-barrel flintlock pocket pistols and flintlock duelling and holster pistols. Shop in London.

**Thomas & Storrs** [about 1800] Shop in London. General gunsmithing.

**Thomason, Edward** [about 1795] General gunsmith in Birmingham. Inventor of a patented frizzle (frizzen) and pan.

**Thompson, Alexander** [about 1780] Shop in Edinburgh, Scotland. Made flintlock fowling pieces and a lightweight cadet flintlock musket.

**Thompson, James** [1810–1835] Under contract with the East India Company, made flintlock muskets. Shop in London.

**Thompson, James** [about 1835] Shop in Penrith, Cumberland. General gunsmith.

Thompson, John [about 1715] General gunsmith in London.

Thompson, W. [about 1815] Shop in Birmingham. General gunsmith.

Thomson, G. [1760–1800] Made screw barrel flintlock pocket pistols. Shop in Edinburgh, Scotland.

Thomson, J. [1800–1830] Shop in London. Made naval flintlock pistols with belt hooks.

Thorn, William [about 1875] Custom gunmaker in London.

Thornton [about 1770] Made flintlock fowling pieces. Shop in London.

Thwaite [1760–1780] Shop at Bath, Somerset. Made double barrel, over and under, flintlock coach pistols and flintlock fowling pieces.

Tilly, E. [about 1690] Shop at Birmingham. General gunsmithing.

Timmings [about 1800] General gunsmith in London.

Timmings, Edward [about 1815] Shop in Birmingham. General gunsmithing.

Tindall & Dutton [1790–1820] Made boxlock flintlock pocket pistols and brass barrel holster pistols. Shop in London.

Tippin [about 1745] Made flintlock muskets with Royal Cypher. Shop in Birmingham.

Tipping [about 1835] Shop at Bath, Somerset. General gunsmithing.

Tipping, J. [about 1840] General gunsmith in London.

Tipping & Lawden [1840–1877] Under Royal Government contract made brass mounted naval percussion pistols. Also made four-barrel metallic cartridge pistols after the Sharps U.S. Patent. Shop in Birmingham.

Tirebuck, Joseph [about 1800] Shop on Haymarket, London. Made flintlock fowling pieces, with silver mountings, of fine workmanship.

Tittensor, John [about 1715] Shop in London. General gunsmithing.

Tocknell [about 1830] General gunsmith at Brighton, Sussex.

Tomes, W. T. [1800–1840] Shop in London. Made cased flintlock duelling pistols with loading accessories. Name changed to Lewis & Tomes 1840 to 1860, and again to Tomes & Co. 1860 to 1884.

Tomlinson [1790–1820] Shop in Dublin, Ireland. Made cased flintlock duelling pistols, and officers' flintlock holster pistols.

Tomlinson & Co. [about 1800] Made double barrel flintlock coach pistols. Shop in Birmingham.

Toope, Robert [about 1745] Made screw barrel flintlock coach pistols with silver mask butt caps. Shop in London.

Tournay, John [about 1715] Shop in London. General gunsmithing.

Tow [1770–1793] Shop in Bond Street, London. Made cased duelling pistols with loading accessories. Under contract with the East India Company made flintlock holster pistols and flintlock carbines.

Tower of London (Royal Armouries) [1339–    ] The three sections of the Tower of London identified as the Armouries are the White Tower, the Bowyer Tower, and the Grand Storehouse or Small Armoury. The latter on the site of the now Waterloo Barracks was completed about 1687 and destroyed by fire in 1841.

The first known record of the Tower as an armory is May 1339, when a Royal Order of Edward III to John de Flete, Keeper of the Tower, to send crossbows to Southampton. These were for an expedition to France before the Battle of the Harbour of Sluys. The following are some interesting notes from the Records of the Tower. In 1485 Sir Richard Guilford of Hempstead, Kent, was appointed by Henry VII first Master of Ordnance. On October 23, 1609, a Royal Warrant to pay Sir Roger Dallison £300 for fitting certain rooms in the Tower for "the keeping and proving of gunpowder." The first date known for the marking of firearms was 1627, when Charles I ordered the Royal Cypher "CR" to be stamped or engraved on all pieces of Royal arms. In 1633 this was changed to a crown over the letter "A." In 1699 the Master of Ordnance, in the reign of William III, ordered the word "Tower" stamped or engraved on all arms ordered or stored there. The Broad Arrow as a mark of Royal Government property was adopted during the reign of George I (1714–1727).

The Master of Ordnance at the Tower ordered and entered into a contract with private firearms makers under given specifications. When these arms had been Proved and Viewed by either the London Proof House, and after 1813 by the Birmingham Proof House, they were delivered to the Tower and then marked "Tower" and became Royal Government property.

It is regrettable that from 1729 to 1855 most of the valuable documents of the Tower Armouries were destroyed. This covered an important era of flintlock and percussion firearms.

**Towle, Thomas** [1690–1714] Shop in London. General gunsmithing.

**Towlson** [about 1840] Made double barrel pill-lock holster pistols. Shop at Newbury, Berkshire.

**Towlson, T.** [1810–1830] Shop at Marlborough, Cheshire. Made flintlock coach pistols.

**Townley, Christopher** [about 1835] Made cased percussion traveling pistols with loading accessories and double barrel percussion sporting guns. Shop at Lancaster.

**Tranter, William** [1853–1885] General gunsmith in Birmingham and later established offices in London. Took out his first Royal Patent in 1853 for a percussion revolver. This revolver had two triggers, one for cocking the hammer and one for firing or double action. For single action used one trigger only. This piece also had a separate loading rod. In 1855 he patented a loading lever attached to the piece. In 1856 he took out an improved patent which eliminated the second trigger and used one trigger for double action. Three models were made: The Dragoon .50 caliber; barrel 7½ or 8 inches; Navy .44 caliber, barrel 5¾ or 6¼ inches; and Pocket .32 caliber, barrel 4½ inches. Tranter received a Royal Government contract in 1858 for the Dragoon and Navy Models. The Dragoon Model also had a detachable carbine stock. In January 1868, he patented his first metallic cartridge revolvers with rod ejector. These were .45 caliber and .38 caliber rim fire.

**Trembley** [about 1810] Made double barrel boxlock flintlock pocket pistols with under spring bayonets. Shop in London.

**Troughton** [about 1780] Shop at Preston, Lancashire. Made flintlock holster pistols with brass mountings.

**Truelocke, Edmund** [1660–1680] Made brass barrel, bell muzzle, flintlock holster pistols. Shop in London.

**Trulock, W.** [1770–1810] General gunsmith in Dublin, Ireland. Name changed to **Trulock & Son,** 9 Dawson Street, Dublin, 1810 to 1861. Made cased percussion traveling pistols with swivel ramrod and loading accessories, also percussion rifles.

**Tucker** [about **1750**] Made Queen Anne–type flintlock coach pistols with brass mask butt caps. Shop in London.

**Turland, E.** [**1702–1714**] Shop in London. General gunsmithing.

**Turner, G.** [about **1850**] Made percussion pepperboxes. Shop in Dublin, Ireland.

**Turner, Henry** [**1840–1862**] General gunsmith in London.

**Turner, John** [about **1810**] Made flintlock coach pistols with spring bayonet. Shop in Birmingham.

**Turner, S.** [**1770–1785**] Made screw barrel boxlock flintlock pocket pistols, also Ferguson-type breech-loading flintlock rifles. Shop in London.

**Turner, S.** [about **1780**] Made cannon barrel flintlock pocket pistols. Shop in Manchester, Lancashire.

**Turner, T.** [about **1830**] Shop in Halifax, Yorkshire. General gunsmith.

**Turner, T.** [about **1840**] General gunsmith at Marlborough, Cheshire.

**Turner, Thomas** [**1861–1879**] Shop at 8 Fisher Street, Birmingham. Made percussion sporting guns. Under Royal Government contract made Army metallic cartridge rifles, Snider Patent.

**Turner, Thomas Henry** [**1840–1860**] Made percussion pepperboxes with silver mountings and cased percussion duelling pistols with loading equipment. Shop at Reading, Berkshire.

**Turney, Henry** [**1864–1871**] General gunsmith in London.

**Turney, J.** [**1820–1832**] Shop in London. General gunsmithing.

**Turney, W.** [about **1750**] Established a gunsmithery in London.

**Turnor** [**1770–1800**] General gunsmith in London.

**Turton, Joseph** [**1813–1857**] Shop in Birmingham. General gunsmith.

**Turvey, Edward** [**1660–1720**] Shop in London. Made combination battle-ax and flintlock pistols. The ax held by the head to fire the pistol. Name changed to **William Turvey** (probably a son or nephew) 1720 to 1760. Made flintlock muskets with Royal Cypher.

**Twigg, T.** [**1760–1780**] A famous gunsmith in London. Made a number of multi-shot flintlock pistols, among these a seven-barrel pepperbox type of flintlock pistol in which the barrels were rotated by hand, also a four-barrel "duck foot" flintlock pistol in which the four barrels were spread out like the fingers of the hand, having one hammer and one flashpan, the four barrels fired at one time. A number of his pistols had an under spring bayonet in which the trigger guard slid back to release the bayonet. He also had a detachable dagger on his pocket pistols. The name was changed to **Twigg & Bass** from 1780 to 1783 and under this name made cased duelling pistols with loading accessories of fine workmanship, also flintlock holster pistols with Royal Cypher. The name reverted to **Twigg** 1783 to 1813 and made officers' flintlock holster pistols of fine workmanship.

**Tyler** [about **1850**] Made percussion pocket pistols. Shop at Melton Mowbray, Leicestershire.

# NOTES
## T

**Unwin & Rodgers** [about 1850] Shop at Sheffield, Yorkshire. Made a combination knife and percussion pistol. The barrel of the pistol along the handle of the knife.

**Upton, William** [1630–1660] Made flintlock (dog-lock) holster pistols and carbines. Shop at Oxford.

**Utting** [1800–1820] Shop in Birmingham. Made double barrel boxlock flintlock pocket pistols.

NOTES

U

**Vanshaw** [about **1745**] General gunsmith in Birmingham.

**Van Wort & Co.** [about **1850**] Made percussion boxlock pocket pistols with folding triggers and saw-handle percussion duelling pistols. Shop in London.

**Van Zaylen, Prosper** [about **1855**] Custom gunmaker in London.

**Vaughan, John** [**1714–1746**] Shop in London. General gunsmithing.

**Veisey & Son** [**1850–1865**] Made percussion double-action revolvers. Shop in Birmingham.

**Venables** [about **1850**] Shop at Oxford. Made cased percussion traveling pistols with loading accessories.

**Vercomb** [**1720–1770**] Shop at Bristol, Gloucestershire. General gunsmithing.

**Vernon** [**1750–1770**] Made flintlock holster pistols. Shop in London.

**Vizer** [about **1770**] Shop in Birmingham. General gunsmithing.

NOTES

V

**Wadsworth, John** [about 1850] Made percussion pocket pistols with folding triggers. Shop in London.

**Wakefield** [about 1820] Shop at Boston, Lincolnshire. Made flintlock fowling pieces of fine workmanship.

**Wakley, M. & W.** [1750–1800] General gunsmiths at Bridgwater, Somerset.

**Waldon, N.** [about 1670] Made brass barrel flintlock blunderbusses. Shop in London.

**Walker** [1690–1739] Shop in London. Made flintlock blunderbusses with Royal Cypher.

**Walker** [about 1830] Shop in Beccles, Suffolk. General gunsmithing.

**Walker, B.** [about 1850] General gunsmith in Birmingham.

**Walker, D.** [1750–1810] Shop at Dumbarton, Scotland. Made all metal flintlock pistols with lobe-shaped butt. His son **Daniel Walker** carried on the shop from 1810 to 1840.

**Walker, J.** [about 1805] Made flintlock dragoon pistols with Royal Cypher. Shop in London.

**Walker, J.** [1800–1830] Shop at Norwich, Norfolk. Made flintlock pistols with belt or sash hook.

**Walker, J.** [about 1790] General gunsmith in Birmingham.

**Walker, James** [about 1720] Established a gunsmithery at Oxford.

**Walker, Richard** [1844–1857] Under Royal Government contract made percussion holster pistols. Shop in Birmingham.

**Walker, William** [about 1630] Established a gunsmithery in Scotland. Location not known.

**Walklate** [about 1810] Made flintlock traveling pistols with under

spring bayonets and flintlock officers' holster pistols of fine workmanship. Shop in London.

**Wall, William** [about 1835] Shop at York. General gunsmithing.

**Wallace** [1800–1840] Made all metal flintlock officers' pistols of fine design and workmanship. Shop at Edinburgh, Scotland.

**Wallace, Samuel** [1750–1780] Shop in Dublin, Ireland, and had own armorer's mark. Made cased flintlock duelling pistols with silver mountings and loading accessories.

**Wallace, Thomas** [about 1795] General gunsmith at Newcastle upon Tyne, Northumberland.

**Waller, James** [about 1775] Shop in London. General gunsmithing.

**Waller, Richard** [about 1715] Established a gunsmithery in London.

**Wallis, G.** [1775–1830] Made boxlock flintlock pocket pistols with silver butt caps, and three-barrel flintlock coach pistols with single hammer and pan, barrels rotated by hand. On some of his pieces the under spring bayonet was released by sliding back the trigger guard. Shop at Hull, Yorkshire.

**Wallis, John** [1859–1874] Custom gunmaker in London.

**Wallis, Stephen** [about 1815] Shop in Birmingham. Made flintlock holster pistols.

**Walls** [about 1800] Made screw barrel flintlock pocket pistols with folding trigger. Shop at Stratford-on-Avon, Warwickshire.

**Walmsley** [about 1780] Made screw cannon barrel flintlock coach pistols. Shop in London.

**Walsh** [1830–1850] Made double barrel, over and under, percussion guns, upper barrel rifled, lower barrel smoothbore. Shop in Dublin, Ireland.

**Walsh, John** [about 1770] Shop at Birmingham. General gunsmithing.

**Walsingham, William** [1730–1779] Made cased pairs of cannon barrel coach pistols with loading accessories. Shop in Birmingham.

**Walters, George** [about 1855] General gunsmith in London.

**Walton, J.** [about 1670] Established a gunsmithery in London.

**Walton, Thomas** [about 1765] General gunsmith in Birmingham.

**Ward** [1800–1830] Shop at Yarmouth, Norfolk. Made flintlock pocket pistols with folding trigger.

**Ward, Henry** [about 1875] Made Webley Patent metallic cartridge revolvers. Shop in Birmingham.

**Ward, Richard** [about 1715] Shop in London. General gunsmithing.

**Ward, T.** [about 1830] General gunsmith at Warrington, Lancashire.

**Ward, William** [about 1765] Shop in Birmingham. General gunsmith.

**Warren, C.** [about 1650] Established a gunsmithery in London.

**Warson, John** [about 1715] General gunsmith in London.

**Waters, John** [1724–1776] Shop in London. Made all metal Scottish-type pistols with scroll butts. These were used to equip the Royal Highland Regiments. Also made flintlock holster pistols. All with Royal Cypher.

**Waters, John** [1767–1781] Made brass cannon barrel flintlock coach pistols and brass barrel, bell muzzle, flintlock pistols. John Waters patented a spring bayonet and release. Shop at

Birmingham. Name changed to **John Waters & Co.** 1781 to 1810.

**Watkin, R.** [1710–1740] Shop in London. Made flintlock holster pistols and flintlock muskets, both with Royal Cypher.

**Watkins & Hill** [1847–1863] Custom gunmakers in London.

**Watmough** [about 1850] General gunsmith at Manchester, Lancashire.

**Watson, Benjamin** [1725–1765] Shop in Birmingham. General gunsmithing.

**Watson, John** [about 1630] One of seven gunsmiths in London whose name appeared in a commission granted by Charles I to make Royal firearms.

**Weatherhead, W.** [about 1840] Made steel barrel percussion blunderbusses. Shop at Derby.

**Webb, Richard** [about 1795] Shop in London. Made brass barrel flintlock officers' holster pistols.

**Webb, W.** [1770–1790] Made brass cannon screw barrel flintlock coach pistols. Shop in London.

**Webley, Philip** [1853–1866] Philip Webley, a gunsmith at Birmingham, took his first patent for a percussion revolver in 1853. This was a single-action revolver with an exceptionally long thumbpiece on the hammer. First models were .44 caliber made with a detachable rammer and in 1855 the rammer was attached to the frame. In October 1857, he patented a double-action, solid frame .44 caliber percussion revolver. During the period from 1853 to 1860 he seems to have sold through dealers with their trade names on the revolvers and the boxes. These were mostly cased and fitted with loading equipment and used as Presentation Pieces. In 1863

Webley took out patents for a breech-loading, side ejector, metallic cartridge, rim-fire revolver. These were .45 caliber and used as side arms by the Royal Irish Constabulary and the Cape Mounted Police. In 1866 the name became **Philip Webley & Son** located at 82 Weaman Street, Birmingham. In 1877 the company bought the C. Preyse Patent of November 1876, for a "break open" or "tip down" model with a barrel latch. This was known as the "Preyse Army Webley" and while never adopted by the Royal Ordnance Board for the Services was popular and used by Army officers. This model was .45 caliber and 5½-inch barrel. In 1882 Webley brought out the Mark I and the only change from the previous model was the improved "stirrup" barrel latch. In 1887 after exhaustive tests this model was adopted by the Ordnance Board as the official arm of the Services. In 1889 the Mark II .476 caliber was brought out known as the "WG" (Webley Government Revolver), and in 1892 the Mark III Model was adopted. This was .455 caliber and built for the cordite cartridge instead of the black powder cartridge. In addition to the army models, pocket models were made of smaller calibers known by the trade names, such as the "British Bull Dog," and the "Metropolitan Police Model." In 1897 Philip Webley & Son merged with W. & C. Scott & Son and became **Webley & Scott Revolver & Arms Co. Ltd.**

**Webster** [about 1825] General gunsmith in London.

**Webster, William** [about 1855] Custom gunmaker in London.

**Weekes** [about 1780] Shop in London. General gunsmithing.

**Welch** [1750–1790] Made flintlock carbines with Royal Cypher. Shop in London.

**Welch** [1800–1820] Shop at Banbury, Oxfordshire. Made double barrel, over and under, flintlock pocket pistols.

**Welch, John** [1767–1780] General gunsmith in Birmingham.

**Wellbourne, George** [about 1840] Shop at Doncaster, Yorkshire. Made percussion pistols with belt hooks.

**Wellford** [about 1750] Made Queen Anne–type flintlock coach pistols with silver mask butt caps. Shop in London.

**Wellington, W.** [about 1840] General gunsmith in London.

**West, John** [about 1690] Shop in Birmingham. General gunsmithing.

**West, Richard** [about 1590] Established a gunsmithery in London.

**Weston, Edward** [1800–1835] Shop at Lewes, Sussex. Made boxlock flintlock pocket pistols.

**Weston, Edward** [1714–1750] Made flintlock duelling pistols. Shop in London.

**Weston, Richard** [about 1700] Shop in Birmingham. Made flintlock holster pistols.

**Weston, W.** [about 1860] Made percussion pepperboxes. Shop at Brighton, Sussex.

**Westwood** [1800–1840] General gunsmith in London.

**Whateley, John & Thomas** [1767–1791] Made flintlock holster pistols. Shop in Birmingham.

**Wheeler, Charles** [about 1855] Custom gunmaker in London.

**Wheeler, Cornelius** [about 1830] General gunsmith at Bridgnorth, Shropshire.

Wheeler, Robert [1767–1813] Shop in London. Made boxlock flintlock pocket pistols with under spring bayonet, and flintlock duelling pistols. Also made brass barrel flintlock blunderbusses. Under Royal Government contract made flintlock holster pistols and musketoons. Had contract with the Hudson's Bay Company for flintlock trade muskets. Name changed to **Robert Wheeler & Son**, 1813 to 1830.

Whistler, Edward [about 1860] Shop at 11 Strand, London. Custom gunmaker and dealer. Had cased percussion revolvers, Tranter Patent, with loading equipment.

White, E. [1850–1888] Custom gunmaker in London.

White, John [about 1715] Established a gunsmithery in London.

Whitehead, Thomas [about 1850] General gunsmith in London.

Whitehouse, John [about 1815] Made double barrel flintlock pocket pistols with under spring bayonet. Shop in Birmingham.

Whitmore, Thomas [about 1870] Custom gunmaker in London.

Whitney, Patrick [about 1810] Shop at Cork, Ireland. Made flintlock duelling pistols.

Whitworth, Sir Joseph [1866–1879] Invented an hexagonal rifled barrel and an hexagonal projectile, also a "solid fluid compressed steel" barrel. Experimental work done at Manchester, Lancashire, and London.

Wicksted [about 1775] Shop in London. General gunsmithing.

Wiggin, John [about 1810] Made screw cannon barrel boxlock flintlock pocket pistols. Shop in London.

Wightman, W. [1820–1835] Shop at Malton, Yorkshire. General gunsmithing.

Wigmore, Jackson [1750–1780] Made officers' flintlock dragoon pistols of fine workmanship. Shop in London.

Wilbraham, George [1815–1854] Shop in London. Made flintlock pocket pistols and flintlock fowling pieces. Later made percussion holster pistols with swivel ramrod and percussion sporting guns. His son **John Wilbraham** carried on the business from 1854 to 1860.

Wilbur [about 1850] Made percussion boxlock pocket pistols with folding triggers. Shop in London.

Wilford, Richard [about 1715] Established a gunsmithery in London.

Wilkes [1770–1814] Shop on St. James Street, London. Made cased flintlock duelling pistols with loading equipment, and flintlock rifles. Name changed to **Wilkes & Harris** above address 1814 to 1850. Made percussion sporting guns.

Wilkin [about 1700] Made flintlock fowling pieces. Shop in London.

Wilkins [about 1820] Shop at Grantham, Lincolnshire. Made flintlock musketoons with Royal Cypher.

Wilkinson [about 1810] General gunsmith at Edinburgh, Scotland.

Wilkinson & Sons, James [1806–1870] Shop at 27 Pall Mall, London. Had Royal Warrant. Made cannon barrel flintlock pocket pistols and under Royal Government contract made naval flintlock boarding pistols. Later, made cased percussion traveling pistols with loading accessories, and percussion sporting guns. Also made percussion pepperboxes and double barrel metallic cartridge .57 caliber "Howdah" pistols for India big-game hunting.

**Wilkinson, T.** [about **1850**] Shop at Cornhill, London. Made percussion pepperboxes.

**Willets** [**1744–1789**] Made flintlock holster pistols and flintlock muskets, both with Royal Cypher. Shops in London and Birmingham.

**Willett** [about **1810**] General gunsmith in Dublin, Ireland.

**Williameson, Gilbert** [about **1635**] Established a gunsmithery in Scotland. Location not known.

**Williams, B.** [**1750–1780**] Made brass barrel flintlock blunderbusses with top spring bayonet. Shop in London.

**Williams, Benjamin** [**1767–1815**] Shop in Birmingham. Made boxlock flintlock pistols.

**Williams, Henry** [**1854–1880**] Custom gunmaker in London.

**Williams, J.** [about **1850**] Made double barrel percussion shotguns. Shop in London.

**Williams, John** [about **1715**] Had a gunsmithery in London. Made iron barrel flintlock blunderbusses.

**Williams & Powell** [**1844–1892**] Shop in Liverpool. Made double barrel, over and under, percussion pocket pistols with folding triggers and cased percussion duelling pistols with loading equipment. Also made percussion pepperboxes and percussion revolvers, Tranter Patent.

**Williamson** [about **1800**] General gunsmith at Hull, Yorkshire.

**Williamson, Robert & William** (brothers) [**1865–1888**] Custom gunmakers in London.

**Willison, Archibald** [about **1870**] Custom gunmaker and importer in London. Imported continental pinfire revolvers.

**Willmore, John** [**1715–1775**] One of the early makers of rifled barrels in England. Shop in London. Made flintlock sporting rifles and cannon barrel flintlock pocket pistols; also brass barrel flintlock blunderbusses.

**Willoughby, R.** [**1775–1790**] Made cannon barrel Queen Anne–type boxlock flintlock pocket pistols. Shop in London.

**Willowes, John** [**1700–1716**] Shop in London. General gunsmithing.

**Wilson** [about **1820**] Shop in Dublin, Ireland. General gunsmithing.

**Wilson, Alexander** [**1810–1835**] Made brass barrel flintlock blunderbusses. Shop in London.

**Wilson, James** [about **1665**] Established a gunsmithery in Scotland. Location unknown.

**Wilson, John** [about **1860**] Made transition percussion revolvers. Shop in London.

**Wilson, R.** [**1720–1750**] Shop in London. Made cannon barrel boxlock flintlock pocket pistols and flintlock holster pistols; also brass barrel flintlock coach blunderbusses.

**Wilson, Richard** [**1767–1780**] General gunsmith in Birmingham. Made multi-shot flintlock pistols with revolving cylinder and firing through a single barrel, probably a prototype of the Elisha Collier revolving pistol.

**Wilson & Co., Thomas** [**1850–1871**] Shops in London and Liverpool. Custom gunmakers, and featured double barrel percussion shotguns.

**Wilson, W. H.** [**1727–1780**] Famous gunsmith in the Minories, London. Made double barrel boxlock flintlock pocket pistols and Queen Anne–type flintlock coach pistols with silver mask butt caps. Under Royal Government

contract made naval flintlock boarding pistols with brass mountings. Also
made flintlock repeating pistols with
a magazine of powder and ball in the
butt stock and operated by a side
lever. Made the Ferguson breech-
loading flintlock rifles.

**Wilson, William** [1760–1820] Made
officers' flintlock holster pistols of fine
workmanship. Also steel barrel flintlock blunderbusses. Shop in London.

**Wing** [1770–1820] Shop at Braintree, Essex. Made screw barrel boxlock flintlock pocket pistols.

**Winsup, John** [about 1715] Shop in
London. General gunsmithing.

**Winter** [about 1810] Made screw
barrel boxlock flintlock pocket pistols.
Shop at Bristol, Gloucestershire.

**Winton, H.** [about 1855] General
gunsmith in Birmingham.

**Wisdon** [about 1790] Shop at Drog-
heda, Ireland. Made cased duelling
pistols with loading accessories.

**Wise** [about 1780] Shop at Bristol,
Gloucestershire. General gunsmithing.

**Wiswold, L.** [about 1830] General
gunsmith at Gainsborough, Lincolnshire.

**Witton, David & William** (brothers) [1854–1869] General gunsmiths
at Birmingham.

**Witton, John** [1840–1849] General
gunsmith in London. Name became
**Witton & Daw** located at 82 Bond
Street and 57 Threadneedle Street,
London, and a shop in Birmingham,
1849 to 1878. Made double barrel percussion pistols and cased percussion
pepperboxes with loading equipment.
Under Royal Government contract
made naval percussion pistols with
belt hook. Also cased percussion revolvers with cleaning and loading
accessories.

**Wogdon** [1760–1797] Shops in London and Dublin, Ireland. Made flintlock coach pistols and flintlock duelling pistols. One of the pairs of pistols at the Alexander Hamilton–Aaron
Burr duel were by Wogdon. Name
changed to **Wogdon & Barton**
(marked pieces London only) 1797
to 1820. Made cased flintlock duelling pistols of fine workmanship. Under Royal Government contract made
flintlock holster pistols and mail coach
carbines.

**Wood, Joseph** [1780–1800] Shop at
York. Made seven-barrel pepperbox
type of flintlock pistols, hand rotated
with a single hammer and one flashpan, also double barrel flintlock
pocket pistols, and brass barrel flintlock blunderbusses with top spring
bayonet. Name changed to **Joseph
Wood & Son** 1800 to 1834.

**Wood, J. W.** [about 1855] Made
cased percussion pepperboxes with
loading equipment. Shop at Manchester, Lancashire.

**Wood, W.** [1800–1840] Shop at
Worcester. Made cased flintlock duelling pistols with loading accessories
and, later, cased percussion duelling
pistols; also percussion sporting guns.

**Woodcock** [about 1800] Made
screw barrel boxlock flintlock pocket
pistols with folding trigger. Shop at
Colchester, Essex.

**Woodley & Sargeant** [about 1815]
General gunsmiths in Birmingham.

**Woodruff** [about 1810] Shop in
London. General gunsmithing.

**Woods** [about 1840] Made boxlock
percussion pocket pistols with folding
trigger. Shop in Birmingham.

**Woods, Edmund** [1864–1891] Custom gunmakers in London.

**Woodward, Thomas** [1863–1880]
Shop in London. Made double barrel

percussion pocket pistols, pin-fire shotguns; and double barrel, derringer-type rim-fire metallic cartridge pistols.

**Wooldridge, R.** [1680–1739] Made flintlock (dog-lock) Grenadiers' muskets with Royal Cypher. Shop in London.

**Wooley** [about 1800] General gunsmith in Bristol, Gloucestershire.

**Wooley & Deakin** [1780–1810] Shop in London. Made double barrel flintlock pocket pistols with top spring bayonet.

**Woolley** [about 1835] General gunsmith in Birmingham.

**Woolloms & Co.** [1867–1882] Custom gunmakers in London.

**Wornall, Thomas** [1654–1689] Made flintlock holster pistols and carbines with Royal Cypher. Shop in London.

**Wright** [about 1830] General gunsmith in Oxford.

**Wright** [about 1835] Shop at Watford, Hertfordshire. General gunsmithing.

**Wright & Co., Charles** [1854–1872] Custom gunmakers in London.

**Wright, H. & J.** [1802–1825] Shop in Birmingham. General gunsmithing.

**Wright, Robert** [1800–1835] General gunsmith in London.

**Wright, Samuel** [about 1830] Shop at Kingston, Surrey. General gunsmith.

**Wright, Thomas** [1714–1752] Shop in London. General gunsmithing.

**Wynne, D.** [1680–1725] Shop in London (used "Londoni" marking on his pieces). Made screw barrel flintlock pocket pistols.

# NOTES
## W

**Yeakell, Henry** [about **1780**] Shop in London. General gunsmithing.

**Yeomans, E.** [**1857–1865**] General gunsmith in London.

**Yeomans, Horace** [**1870–1888**] Custom gunmaker in London.

**Yeomans, J.** [**1820–1850**] Shop in London. General gunsmithing.

**York, Charles** [**1810–1830**] General gunsmith in London.

**Young** [about **1775**] Made officers' light flintlock muskets. Shop in London.

**Younge** [**1830–1860**] Shop at Bury, Lancashire. Made officers' percussion holster pistols.

NOTES

Y

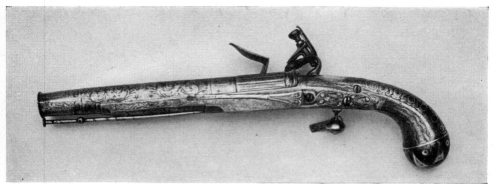

## SCOTTISH FLINTLOCK PISTOL
Made by JAMES MURDOCH of Inverness, Scotland, about 1720.

## ENGLISH CANNON BARREL FLINTLOCK
Made by WILLIAM GRICE of London, about 1740.

E

KETLAND FLINTLOCK BOXLOCK PISTOL

Mark on one side of lockplate: "KETLAND & CO"; on the other side: "LONDON"; both in gold inset. On barrel: London proof and view marks, both in gold inset. Made

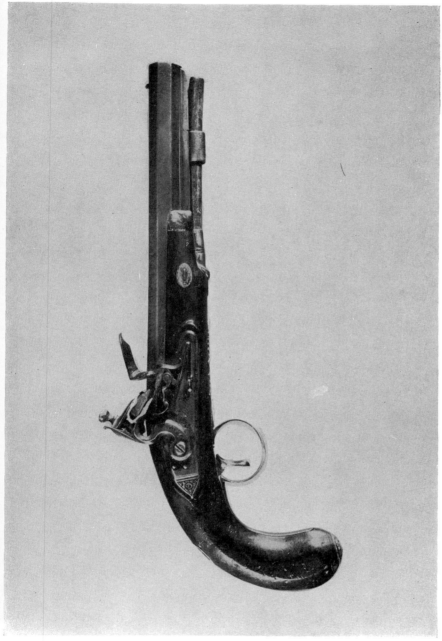

WALLACE FLINTLOCK DUELLING PISTOL

Mark on lockplate: "WALLACE." On barrel: "WALLACE DUBLIN"; also Dublin proof and view marks and maker's mark between proof marks "SW" in rectangle. Made about 1750.

E *

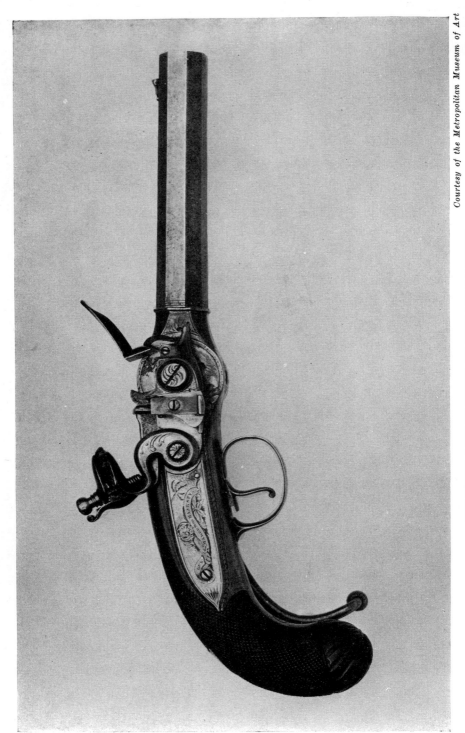

ENGLISH MULTI-SHOT FLINTLOCK PISTOL
Made by H. W. MORTIMER of London, about 1800.

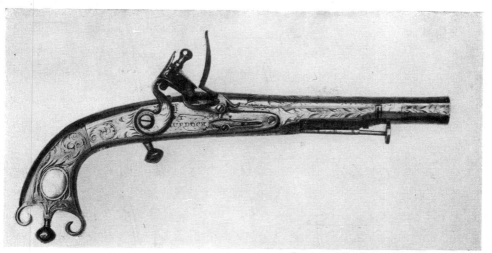

### SCOTTISH FLINTLOCK PISTOL
Made by THOMAS MURDOCH of Leith, Scotland, about 1750.

### ENGLISH DOUBLE BARREL FLINTLOCK PISTOL
Made by JOSEPH EGG of London, about 1820.

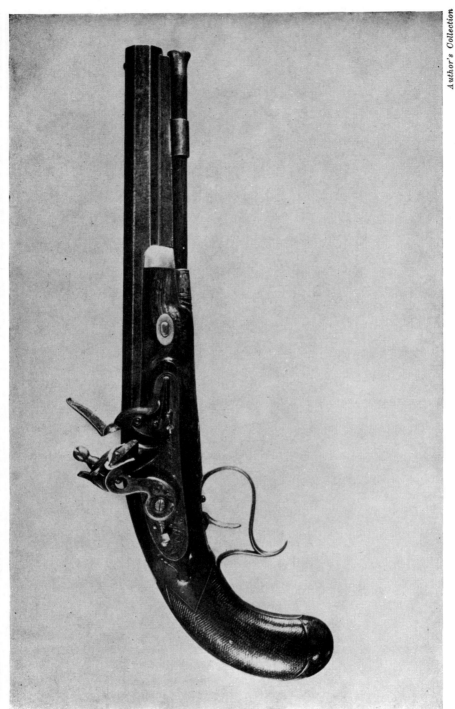

STEPHENS FLINTLOCK PISTOL

Mark on lockplate: "J. STEPHENS." On barrel: "J. STEPHENS MAKER QUEEN STREET BRYANSTON SQUARE LONDON." London proof and view marks on barrel. Made about 1820.

BEATTIE PERCUSSION PISTOL

Mark on lockplate: "J. BEATTIE." On barrel: "J. BEATTIE 205 REGENT STREET LONDON"; also on barrel, London proof and view marks. Made about 1835.

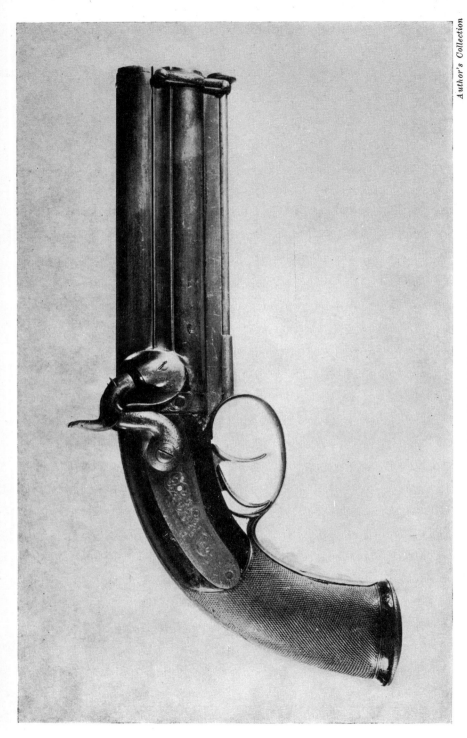

LACY PERCUSSION DOUBLE BARREL PISTOL

Mark on lockplate: "LACY & CO." On barrel: "LACY & CO LONDON"; also London proof and view marks. Made about 1840.

# NOTES

A. Due to the fact that the letters I and J in the old English Script are so similar, it is sometimes difficult to determine the initial of the maker's name on the piece.

B. Regarding the span of years a firearms maker was active, I have been conservative on the available data, and there may be a possibility of "before and after" in the years shown.

C. Where the name of the town is the county seat, the shire is not given.

D. Where the types of arms are given, these are now known to be in existence. Without question the maker made many other arms and the early makers were in all probability general gunsmiths as well.

E. Approximate over-all length of the various classifications of English pistols:

| | |
|---|---|
| Pocket | 5 to 7 inches |
| Greatcoat | 8 to 11 inches |
| Traveling or Coach | 13 to 15 inches |
| Duelling | 15 to 18 inches |
| Holster or Dragoon | 16 to 21 inches |

F. Approximate periods of the types of butt on Scottish pistols:

| | |
|---|---|
| 1575–1650 | Fishtail butt (Highlanders) Snaphaunce lock |
| 1640–1750 | Lobe or lemon butt (Lowlanders) Snaphaunce or Flintlock |
| 1650–1750 | Heart-shaped butt (Lowlanders) Flintlock |
| 1690–1850 | Scroll or Ramshorn butt (Highlanders) Flintlock and Percussion lock |

G. The "Brown Bess" Musket: This famous flintlock musket was designed and developed for the British Army during the reign of Queen Anne (1702–1714) and was the prototype of all Service muskets up to percussion period 1834, when the Board of Ordnance first conducted tests of the percussion system. The complete turnover to percussion was accomplished in 1842. The "Brown Bess" was chosen by John Churchill, Duke of Marlborough, then Captain-General of the British Troops at home and abroad and Master-General of

Ordnance. It had the qualities of the most perfect military musket of the times and a vast improvement over the Infantry arms that preceded it, both in the British Armies and the armies on the Continent. The musket weighed about 12 pounds and the barrel of the original "Brown Bess" was 46 inches long and had a caliber of .77 to .80. The stock was of walnut and stained a reddish brown, the barrel itself was browned or russeted by a process of artificial oxidation or pickling in an acid bath, hence affectionately called by the soldiers "Brown Bess." (There is another school who claim the derivation of the name came from the "Brown Bill," a staff with a knife blade fitted on the top and painted brown. Before firearms these were carried by pikemen and when they got muskets they called them "Brown Bess.") The mounts were of brass with 4 ramrod pipes, trigger guard, and heavy butt plate. The lock itself was much improved over the former locks and known as a bridle lock. Another great improvement was the bayonet which was attached to the muzzle of the barrel by a steel collar or socket which fitted over the outside of the barrel, and the triangular blade was offset to permit firing the piece with the bayonet attached. Previously the bayonet was jammed in the muzzle of the barrel and prevented its use as a firearm.

H. Flints: The art of chipping, or as it is termed "knapping," flint is probably one of the oldest industries in England. In neolithic times the inhabitants of the British Isles went to the chalk and flint deposits of Brandon to obtain material for their arrowheads, knives, spearheads, and other primitive weapons and tools. The Brandon quarries are about eighty-six miles north of London in Suffolk. In 1686 the Royal Government established the making of gunflints at Brandon, and until 1835 these quarries were the source of all flints used by the British Government. Even after the percussion lock supplanted the flintlock, gunflints were made for use in Africa, Spain, Italy, and India until 1900. The "knappers" reckoned or sold their flints by the thousand. The flints were packed in half casks, each of which would hold 2000 musket flints or 3000 carbine flints or 4000 pistol flints. The Hudson's Bay Company trade lists issued in 1748 give 16 to 20 flints as the barter limit for 1 beaver pelt. Within the past few years there are about 6 "flint knappers" in Brandon who supply the world trade for museums and collectors of flintlock firearms.

I. The Gunmakers Company (London): A Royal Charter was granted by Charles I on March 14, 1637, to the "Master Wardens and Society of the Mystery of Gunmakers of the City of London" which was later known as The Gunmakers Company. The power granted under this Charter was very broad for it stated "The divers black-smiths and others unexpert in the art of gunmaking had taken upon them to make, try and prove guns after their unskillful way, whereby the Trade was not only much damnified but much harm and danger through such unskillfulness had happened to His Majesty's Subjects." It further authorized The Gunmakers Company to "search for and prove all manner of hand guns, great and small, daggs and pistols and every part thereof, whether made in London (City) or within 10 miles thereof or imported from foreign ports, or otherwise brought hither for sale." In 1672 a second Royal Charter was granted by Charles II to The Gunmakers Company which empowered it to enforce the proving of all arms then in use and for sale in all of England. This did much to stop the importation of untried firearms or barrels.

The Proof House was established outside of the City of London on Commercial Road and conveniently located on the border of the Minories, which was the center of the gunmaking trade and also within a short distance from the Tower of London to which Royal arms made under Government contract by the Minories firearms makers were delivered after proving.

The proving consisted of two operations. First the rough barrels were loaded with a double charge of powder and double the weight of ball; after firing, if the barrel did not burst or rupture, it was stamped with the first Proof Mark—the Crown over the letter "V," indicating the barrel had been "viewed" and tested in the rough. The second operation was proving the finished barrel with a double charge of powder and twice the weight of ball. If this test was satisfactory the barrel was stamped with the letters "GP" (Gunmakers Proof) under a Crown, which was the mark that the barrel or chamber had been proved in the finished state. In the method of proving, the barrels were clamped in racks with the muzzles pointing at a bank of sand. From 20 to 50 were fired at once with a train of powder running across the touchholes.

J. The Guardians of the Birmingham Proof House: Firearms marked London were considered superior to those marked Birmingham in quality and brought a better price on the market and some Birmingham firearms makers marked their pieces "London." In 1813 the Gunmakers Company of London petitioned for a bill in the House of Commons compelling every manufacturer of firearms to mark them with his name and place of fabrication. This roused the Birmingham makers and they formed a Guild, "The Guardians of the Birmingham Proof House" and established their own proof house and proof mark. Ketland was active in this movement and the Birmingham Proof Mark was a derivation of his private armourer's mark that he had used. The view mark was crossed scepters with a crown in top segment and the letter "V" the lower segment. The proof mark was crossed scepters with the letter "B" in the left-hand quadrant, the crown in the top quadrant and the letter "C" in the right-hand quadrant and the letter "P" in the bottom quadrant.

# SCHEDULE OF GUN PROOF MARKS
# REGISTERED IN ENGLAND

### THE GUNMAKERS COMPANY, LONDON

### THE GUARDIANS OF THE BIRMINGHAM
### PROOF HOUSE

Issued by Order of the Authorities of the London and Birmingham
Proof Houses

# *APPENDIX*

## CHRONOLOGY OF ENGLISH, IRISH, AND SCOTTISH FIREARMS

**1485:** Sir Richard Guilford of Hempstead, Kent, appointed by Henry VII first Master of Ordnance at the Tower of London.

**1585:** Earliest known all metal snaphaunce pistol made by Alison at Dundee, Scotland.

**1627:** First stamping of Royal arms, when Charles I ordered the letters **"CR"** on all arms.

**1629:** Seven London gunsmiths granted a commission by Charles I to make Royal arms.

**1635:** Harman Barne of London made the earliest known breech-loading flint-lock rifle.

**1637:** The first charter was granted by Charles I on March 14, 1637, to the Gun-makers Company of London, establishing the London Proof House and Proof Marks.

**1646:** Thomas Caddell established the first gunsmithery at Doune, Perthshire, Scotland.

**1686:** The Royal Government took over the quarries at Brandon for the chip-ping or "knapping" of flints.

**1699:** The Master of Ordnance at the Tower of London ordered the word **"Tower"** stamped or engraved on all Royal firearms inspected and stored there.

**1700** (circa): John Cookson of London developed a practical and workable re-peating flintlock pistol.

**1710** (circa): The first "Brown Bess" flintlock muskets were issued to the British Army.

**1776:** A Crown Patent dated December 2, 1776, was isssued to Major Patrick Ferguson for a breech-loading flintlock rifle.

**1802:** The 95th Regiment, later called the Rifle Brigade, were issued flintlock rifles, made under Royal Government contract by Ezekiel Baker.

**1807:** The Reverend Alexander John Forsyth granted a Crown Patent on July 4, 1807, for his percussion lock.

**1811:** Elisha Hayden Collier received his Crown Patent for a revolving cylinder firearm.

**1811:** Royal Armoury at Enfield established.

**1813:** The Guardians of the Birmingham Proof House at Birmingham formed and the Proof House established.

**1815:** Royal Armoury at Enfield used as a depot; manufacturing ceased.

**1816:** Joseph Manton of London patented his percussion "tube lock."

**1834:** The Board of Ordnance conducted the first tests of the percussion system of firing.

**1836:** The first percussion muskets were issued to the 3rd Grenadier and the 1st Coldstream Guard Regiments.

**1841:** First percussion muskets used by the second battalion of the 55th Regiment of Infantry in actual battle. On August 26, 1841, in the action at Amoy during the First China War.

**1851:** The percussion rifle issued to the British Infantry with the Minié bullet.

**1851:** Robert and John Adams patented a percussion revolver.

**1852:** Samuel Colt established his London plant in May at Besborough Place, Thames Bank.

**1855:** Royal Armoury at Enfield again became a manufacturing arsenal.

# REIGNS OF ENGLAND

| | |
|---|---|
| Edward III | 1327–1377 |
| Richard II | 1377–1399 |
| Henry IV | 1399–1413 |
| Henry V | 1413–1422 |
| Henry VI | 1422–1461 |
| Edward IV | 1461–1483 |
| Richard III | 1483–1485 |
| Henry VII | 1485–1509 |
| Henry VIII | 1509–1547 |
| Edward VI | 1547–1553 |
| Mary | 1553–1558 |
| Elizabeth I | 1558–1603 |
| James I | 1603–1625 |
| Charles I | 1625–1649 |
| The Commonwealth | 1649–1660 |
| Charles II | 1660–1685 |
| James II | 1685–1688 |
| ⎰ Mary II | 1688–1694 |
| ⎱ William III | 1688–1702 |
| Anne | 1702–1714 |
| George I | 1714–1727 |
| George II | 1727–1760 |
| George III | 1760–1820 |
| George IV | 1820–1830 |
| William IV | 1830–1837 |
| Victoria | 1837–1901 |

# BIBLIOGRAPHY

*Armouries of the Tower of London, vols. I & II,* by Charles J. Ffulkes.
*Arms and Armament,* by Charles J. Ffulkes.
*Arms and Armour,* by J. G. Waller.
*Arms and Armour in Antiquity and the Middle Ages,* by Charles Bontell.
American Art Association Catalogues (New York).
Anderson Galleries Catalogues (New York).
*Journal of the American Military Institute* (Washington, D.C.).
*Journal of the Society for Army Historical Research* (London).
Francis Bannerman Sons Catalogues (New York).
*British Pistols and Guns 1640–1840,* by Ian Glendening.
Brooklyn Museum Arms Catalogues (Brooklyn, New York).
*History of Birmingham,* by Conrad Gill and Charles Grant Robertson.
Christie, Matson & Woods Catalogues (London).
*Deanes' Manual of the History and Science of Firearms.*
*English Pistols and Revolvers,* by J. N. George.
*English Guns and Rifles,* by J. N. George.
*European Arms and Armor,* by Stephen V. Grancsay.
*European Hand Firearms of the 16th, 17th, and 18th Centuries,* by Herbert J. Jackson.
Edinburgh Castle Museum Arms Catalogues (Edinburgh).
*The Reverend Alexander John Forsyth and His Invention of the Percussion Lock,* by Maj. Gen. Sir Alexander Forsyth Reid.
*History of Firearms,* by Maj. H. P. C. Pollard.
*The Guns,* by Sir James Emerson Tennent.
*The Gun and Its Development,* by W. W. Greener.
*Gun Collecting,* by Charles Edward Chapel.
Kimball Arms Company Catalogues (Woburn, Massachusetts).
Metropolitan Museum of Art, Arms Catalogues (New York).
*The Military Opinions of General Sir John Fox Burgoyne, Bart.,* Collected and edited by Captain George Wrottesley.
*Journal of the Company of Military Collectors and Historians,* Washington, D.C.
*The Rudolph J. Nunnemacher Collection Milwaukee Museum* (2 vols.), by John Metschl.
Parke-Bernet Galleries Catalogues (New York).
*Pistols, Their History and Development,* by James Frith.

*Proof Tests and Proof Marks*, by Lt. Col. Calvin Goddard.
*Pepperbox Firearms*, by Lewis Winant.
*Remarks on Rifle Guns*, by Ezekiel Baker.
*The Revolver, Its Description, Management and Use*, by Patrick Edward Dove.
*The Westley Richards Firm, A Brief History.*
Sotheby Catalogues (London).
*Scottish Hand Firearms*, by Charles E. Whitelaw.
*Stand and Deliver, The Story of Highwaymen*, by Patrick Pringle.
*The Story of Colt's Revolver*, by William B. Edwards.
Royal United Service Museum Catalogues (London).
Victoria and Albert Museum Arms Catalogue (London).
Wallace Collection Arms Catalogues (London).
Wallis & Wallis Catalogues (Lewes, England).
Walpole Galleries Catalogues (New York).
*Yankee Arms Maker*, by Jack Rohan.